Passive Income

40 Ideas to Launch Your Online Business Including Blogging, Ecommerce, Dropshipping, Photography, Affiliate Marketing and Amazon FBA

The information herein is offered for informational purposes solely, and is universal as so. The presentation of the information is without contract or any type of guarantee assurance.

The trademarks that are used are without any consent, and the publication of the trademark is without permission or backing by the trademark owner. All trademarks and brands within this book are for clarifying purposes only and are the owned by the owners themselves, not affiliated with this document.

Table of Contents

INTRODUCTION

I have always wanted to write a book on these ideas. The ideas mentioned in this book have been tested and proven either by myself, or by others I know.

People say that ideas rule the world, and they're not kidding.

There is always that million dollar idea lurking in the shadows. We have in this dot com age seen a lot of businesses starting out in garages and going on to become multi-billion dollar corporations, all in less than 20 years. Most great things started with an idea, virtually everything around us started with an idea. All the inventors did was ask the right questions and push towards achieving their set objectives. My goal is to unleash the creativity inside of you, to get you out of that comfort zone to that place where you can change things. It is my earnest desire that when you read through this guide, you will find your own idea!

I also know that sometimes, there is always that need for a little extra to get you going and that's why I have put together this guide on 40 ideas to help you generate income.

Some of the ideas listed here are passive, while others will require a greater amount of time and dedication to see them through. However, all of them can eventually become passive through outsourcing. Some will require skills you already possess and for others, you will have to take a few courses and work at it to gain mastery before setting up a business in that niche.

In this guide, I will show you in simple steps how to generate income online in a wide variety of businesses, and all of them from the comfort of your home. The language is intentionally conversational and easy to follow.

Note: these ideas are not get-rich-quick schemes. Almost all of them require hard work initially but you can eventually outsource a lot of tasks. For some of the ideas, you can turn the online business into passive income all by yourself. For others, you will need help from others to create that passive income that you need.

Happy reading!

CHAPTER 1 - BLOGGING

While blogs are now so commonplace that it's near impossible not to have come across one yet, for the purpose of this guide, we shall be discussing: 1) what blogs are, 2) how you can make money from blogging, and 3) how you can setup your own blog and be on your way to financial freedom in 2017.

So what exactly is a blog?

A weblog, shortened to blog, though similar to a website, is a journal/diary that is usually maintained by one person called the blogger. Usually, blogs can be categorized into niches (fashion, travel, entertainment etc.). The particular niche determines the content and this reflects the passion of the blogger. Bloggers are usually very passionate about the niche they write about.

Quality content (blog posts) is the fundamental piece of every blog. To ensure your blog gets lots of visitors—because you need to have people visiting and reading your blog posts to make it popular and in turn make money—you have to regularly create content (blog posts). Depending on the niche, your content should be trendy, catchy (you can use lots of pictures) and engaging. You are expected to update your blogs often to maintain readership.

Getting Started

Here are the definitions of a few words that will appear regularly in the course of this guide.

Blog (n.) – A blog is an online journal or diary that is available on the Internet.

Blogger (n.) – A blogger is an individual who is the blog

owner or a person who is responsible for creating content or posts.

Blog Post (n.) – An article or writing that is inside the blog. This is content that keeps the readers coming back again.

Blogging (v.) – Is the act of maintaining or writing a blog

Blogging is quite an engaging venture. In a featured article "the Billionaire Bloggers" on forbes.com, it is stated that more than 112 million people in the world blog regularly and there are 13 billionaires out of the 1,125 on the list who are true bloggers. Even billionaires are bloggers...so why not you?

Blogging, as a profession, has proven to be very lucrative. However, not many people have the knowledge and understanding to make a successful career out of blogging. Although creating a very successful blog is no easy feat, as the blogosphere is quite competitive, with a good measure of passion, talent, dedication and good business sense, you can become very successful.

There is a need for bloggers to have a drive, passion and expertise in their respective niches to be successful.

However, most of the money made by bloggers doesn't usually come directly from just blogging. A blog mostly serves as a platform or springboard to launch other products and services that bring in income. There is no method of making money that is better than the other; they all provide endless possibilities for the blogger. All you have to do is to find a combination that works for you, or create your own. The key to making good money from blogging is to have multiple streams of income from your blog. For instance, if you blog about travelling, then try selling your service as a booking agent or create an affiliate with travel agencies, hotels or

Airbnb.

How to Make Money from Blogging

There are lots of ways you can make money from blogging. The ways listed below are just a few. Your reach and readership are the major things that will determine how much you can make, as your window of opportunity is endless when your blog becomes very popular.

Google AdSense: Google AdSense is the most popular way of creating income through blogging. Google AdSense is the ad network powered by Google and it is probably the most popular ad network in the world. Most of the ads you come across when you surf the web are placed on the website or blogs by Google AdSense.

Google AdSense ads come in various shapes and forms; some can be images and others text. They are placed in headers, footers or within posts, and anywhere else the blog owner chooses to display them. AdSense is a good place to start for new bloggers because it is easy to set up. Advertisers pay money for clicks on their ads that are displayed on your blog. The key here to reaping lots of benefit from Google AdSense is to create good content and drive as much traffic as you can to your blog. The more people who visit your blog, the greater the likelihood is of them clicking on the ads.

Sponsored Posts: This is one of the most effective ways that you can make money from your blog through advertising. A sponsored post is a blog post that you are asked to make by a company or organization that is trying to reach readers of your blog. In this type of post, you are most likely commissioned to write about a service or product. You are expected to show the service or product in a good light so as to encourage your blog readers to consider buying from the company or organization. It is a good practice to be upfront and clear to your readers on your relationship with the company. It helps to maintain your integrity.

Note: Keep sponsored posts to a minimum as it can be offensive to some readers.

Private Ads: Private ads are unique ads that are not routed through Ad networks. They are a direct partnership between you, the blogger and the business advertising on your blog. Initial contact can be made by the blogger or by the advertiser. Be clear on what's expected by both parties. Not sure what to charge? Look around to see what others in your niche charge. You can often find this information on a blog's advertising page or media kit. Not sure of how to get adverts? There are ways to reach out to your target companies and one of those ways is to visit similar blogs in your niche and see what's being advertised there. Contact those companies and who knows, you may just receive a cheque in the mail.

Affiliate Marketing: The job of an affiliate marketer is to promote someone else's product or service in a blog post or through other means. When you create links on your post to that product or service using your unique affiliate link or code, you get paid a commission when someone clicks on that link and makes a purchase (or completes a desired action set by the company). Affiliate marketing is quite popular among bloggers because of the numerous companies out there who are looking to advertise their products. For instance, if your niche is sports, you can set up affiliate accounts on the various online sports betting websites and create affiliate links to those websites in your blog post.

Sell a product: This is another great way to monetize your blog. The easiest way to monetize your blog is to sell a product or service. You can do this directly by embedding images of the product and a button that says "buy now". You will want to mention the price but only after a well-written sales copy. It is a good idea to include "bonuses" if possible. This is mostly done when selling digital products such as courses or ebooks. There are basically two types of products you can sell on your blog; physical products and digital products.

Physical Products: Platforms like Shopify and Woo Commerce have made it cheaper than ever for anyone to create an online store to sell physical products online. Selling physical products online may be a bit difficult due to the various logistics involved but you can find companies that offer white label or drop shipping services, which frees up your time for driving traffic and creating quality content.

Digital Products: If you can't deal with the challenge of selling physical products, you can opt for selling digital products; how-to videos, recipes, hacks, training courses, or even software, all of which can be delivered electronically. For instance, Brian Dean, internet marketer and SEO guru, runs a successful SEO membership site called SEOThatWorks.com. He tutors people on how to make their website or blog such that it is optimized for search engines. It costs about $2000 to join, and he has had many happy members as part of his program.

How to Setup Your Blog

If you are convinced about the prospects of blogging, then you should give it a try. First off, before building your blog, you have to decide on the name and niche you would like to blog about. The trick here is to first find your passion. This will be necessary in the long run because you want to blog about something you know well. You will have to continuously post updates or new things, and the only way to really stay on top of that is to be motivated through your passions. Once that is taken care of, you should pick a name that is catchy, easy to pronounce and available for domain registration.

The next step is to install Word Press and design your theme and layout. Most web hosting companies offer pre-set themes and layouts on Word Press for bloggers. If you have no knowledge of website design, I would suggest you make use of the hosting sites that offer a "one click" Word Press setup for you. There are various platforms like Wix and Bluehost that offer such features. Then, install plugins to allow for sharing of your posts. This allows readers to share your blog posts on major social media platforms like Facebook and twitter. It gives you more visibility and would help drive traffic to your blog.

Finally, create great content. Compelling content will keep the blog visitor coming back and will encourage sharing of your posts, which will ultimately drive traffic to your blog! Make sure you write and publish regularly, make great use of your network to promote your blog and who knows, you may just be on your way to becoming the next Mashable or TechCrunch.

I would advise you to check out Forbes list of the world top 10 richest bloggers for some inspiration and wisdom.

CHAPTER 2 – AMAZON FBA

Amazon FBA (Fulfilled by Amazon) has become very popular, especially since 2014. This business model is geared towards physical products only, the categories of which will be mentioned later below. Perhaps the reason for its popularity comes from the fact that anyone can sell their physical products online, without having to be a business person necessarily. A lot of the risk is removed, as Amazon handles all of the inventory storage, shipping and customer service. This is a great advantage because one does not need to take the risk of opening a warehouse, whereas a traditional business owner would not have this luxury. Furthermore, Amazon is very popular and it has lots of traffic already, so finding customers is made easier. Statistics show that 44% of all ecommerce happens on Amazon. That is huge considering other popular online stores such as Wal-Mart, Target, and eBay are also trying to sell their products online.

While both of the advantages of not needing a warehouse and not worrying too much about traffic are great, there are fees associated with this service that Amazon provides. The rule of thumb is that Amazon FBA will take about 1/3 of the selling price of your product. However, the fees vary depending on how large and how heavy your product is. There are several sizing categories such as small standard size, large standard size, small oversize, medium oversize, large oversize and special oversize. Each of the dimensions of these sizes can be found on the Amazon website. Furthermore, if the product is heavier than 20 lbs, then it is considered to be oversized.

Amazon Categories

The physical product categories are listed below. It is important to note that Amazon is continuously making changes and may add or remove a category.

Amazon Device Accessories
Amazon Kindle
Automotive & Powersports
Baby Products (Excluding Apparel)
Beauty
Books
Business Products (B2B)
Camera & Photo
Cell Phones
Clothing & Accessories
Collectible Coins
Electronics (Accessories)
Electronics (Consumer)
Fine Art
Grocery & Gourmet Food
Handmade
Health & Personal Care
Historical & Advertising Collectibles
Home & Garden
Industrial & Scientific
Luggage & Travel Accessories
Music
Musical Instruments
Personal Computers
Professional Services
Shoes, Handbags & Sunglasses
Software & Computer Games
Sports
Sports Collectibles
Sports Collectibles
Tools & Home Improvement
Tools & Home Improvement
Toys & Games
Video Games & Video Game Consoles
Video, DVD, & Blu-Ray
Watches
Wine

Out of these, there are certain "restricted" categories and not everyone can sell products belonging to these categories. Below is a list of 22 restricted categories that require approval from Amazon before sellers can sell corresponding products. Amazon may make changes to them, so it is important to double check the categories on the Amazon website before you launch a product online. To gain access to these categories, Amazon has an approval process which often involves providing invoices and other documentation to Amazon. I would suggest that you avoid these categories if you are launching your product for the first time.

Automotive & Powersports
Beauty
Clothing & Accessories
Collectible Books
Collectible Coins
Entertainment Collectibles
Fine Art
Gift Cards
Grocery & Gourmet Foods
Health & Personal Care
Independent Design
Jewelry
Luggage & Travel Accessories
Major Appliances
Services
Sexual Wellness
Shoes, Handbags & Sunglasses
Sports Collectibles
Textbook Rentals
Video, DVD, & Blu-ray
Watches
Wine

Getting Started

There are many ways to sell on Amazon FBA including Retail Arbitrage, Online Arbitrage and Private Labeling. Retail Arbitrage is basically the practice of buying cheap products from big block stores or thrift stores and selling them online under existing Amazon listings. Online Arbitrage is the practice of buying products online from other websites such as eBay and selling them on Amazon to make a profit.

It is important to note that Amazon has made it a lot harder for people to sell through Retail and Online Arbitrage because it is catering more towards brands. Therefore, it is probably best to avoid these two methods and go for the third option of Private Labeling. Private Labeling requires more work but has a lot of advantages. Firstly, you can create your own listing for your product, since it is for your own brand. This gives you leverage because others cannot sell your branded product unless you give them permission to do so. Secondly, as your brand grows, you can add more products and have a real business of your own. In any case, the remaining section of this chapter will focus on Private Labeling.

There are essentially four steps to launching your own private label product: Product Research, Setting up Your Seller Central Account, Finding a Supplier, and Product Launch.

Product Research

Not every product will sell well on Amazon. After selecting your category, you will need to look at existing products on Amazon before you can select a product of your own. To figure out demand for a product, you will need to look at the BSR (Best Seller Rank). The BSR is located on the listing page of almost every product on Amazon under the "Product Detail" section. A BSR of 10 would mean that product is selling a lot, maybe hundreds of units per day; while a BSR of 100,000 would mean that the product is not selling well at all.

The other thing to look for is the number of reviews of existing products on Amazon. If your competition has 1,000+ reviews and multiple brands have high reviews, then it is a good idea to avoid such a product. This is because when you launch your product, you will only have a few reviews. Most of the buyers on Amazon look at reviews before buying so your sales will be low.

There is software that make product research easier. One of the most popular of such software is Jungle Scout. On their website, there is a free tool called Jungle Scout Estimator. You basically select a category and enter a BSR, after which it will display the number of units being sold per month. It is a good idea to check and see how many sales your competitors are getting per day before you launch your product. Jungle Scout also has some paid tools you can use that will give you additional information such as estimated monthly revenue, FBA fees, number of reviews, number of sellers, etc.

The two main points to keep in mind are that you are looking for a product with low reviews and a low BSR (which means high sales). It may be frustrating but eventually you will find a product you like. I would advise to go for a product that is relatively lightweight, because heavy products have their own issues. Normally you want to look for a product that weighs between 0.5 to 2 lbs. The price will also matter because if it is too low, then your profit margin will also be low, and can even lead to loss upon launch. The price range should be between 15 and 60 dollars for standard sized products, but you can target higher prices if your product is heavy or very large. A good tool to use is the Amazon FBA Calculator, which will show you the FBA fees the existing sellers are paying to sell their products. You can simply enter an ASIN (a unique Amazon listing identifier) and Amazon will provide all of the details.

It will take a week or more to find the product you are satisfied with. It is important to stay patient and not become frustrated, as many products will either have too many reviews, or the BSRs may not be great, or the price might be too low. In the end, once you have your product, it is time to move on to the next step.

Setting Up Your Seller Account

To set up your seller account, you will need to go to Sellercentral.amazon.com. After arriving here, you will need to provide basic information such as name, email and address. Once you have your login, you will be presented with two options. You can either choose a professional selling plan or an individual selling plan. The professional plan has a monthly fee depending on which online country you are selling on (i.e. Amazon.com, Amazon.ca, Amazon.de, Amazon.co.uk, etc). For Amazon.com in USA, the fee is $40 per month and other platforms have similar professional selling fees. These fees are for your seller account and should not be confused with FBA fees, which are related to your product.

For a private label product that you are trying to launch, you will likely need a professional plan. Therefore, you will need a credit card so that Amazon can charge you the monthly fee. It is important to note that you will be charged a monthly fee regardless of whether you make any sales or not. You will also need to provide banking information so that Amazon can deposit the revenue from your sales into your bank account.

Not all bank accounts from different countries are supported, but many countries have been incorporated by Amazon including Canada, UK, Germany and others. After your basic information has been inputted, it is time to move on to finding a supplier.

Finding a Supplier

The most popular website to find a supplier is Alibaba.com. Most of the suppliers on here are Chinese but other countries are also available. You will need to contact many suppliers for the product of your choice because not everyone will reply. Since China has a different time zone, it will likely be night there while it is daytime in North America. As such you will likely be corresponding every 24 hours. To filter your suppliers, you can select many options including "gold supplier" and "trade assurance." These checks are put on Alibaba to ensure that you do not get scammed by anyone. Once you are ready to contact the suppliers, it is a good idea to ask them the following questions:

1) What is the minimum order quantity?

2) Can you label this product with my brand name?

3) How many days will it take to produce X amount of units?

4) What is your quote for door to door shipping from China to the Amazon warehouse in the USA (or whichever marketplace you are selling on) using UPS, DHL or FedEx?

5) What is the weight and size of one product?

6) How many days will it take to ship the products once

they are ready?

7) Can you make special packaging if we provide the package design files?

After a few days, you will begin to receive responses. It is important to look at the price, lead time and reputation of the supplier. The lead time is usually around 1 month but if you see something like 2 or 3 months, you may want to ask the supplier to reduce it as much as possible. The most important thing to decide at this stage is whether you will be able to make a profit after subtracting FBA fees (which you can get from the Amazon FBA calculator through a simple Google search), shipping costs and product costs. If the costs are too high, it may be a good idea to return to the product selection stage. The payment terms will also be important. Normally you want to pay 30% down payment and then 70% after production is complete (but before your supplier ships to the Amazon warehouse). In any case, once you are satisfied with the data you have, you can choose a supplier.

The selected supplier will likely need the shipping address, as well as your billing information. The shipping address will come from your Amazon seller account once you create a "shipping plan" online. Amazon will ask you to input the supplier name, address and the number of units you will be shipping. Once that is complete, you will be provided with a PDF file that contains Shipping Labels and also the shipping address. This file and information will then go to your supplier.

Product Launch

While you are waiting for your products to be manufactured, you can work on things such as your Amazon listing images, keywords, and description. All three of these things are important because they will ultimately decide if customers want to buy your product or not. You can outsource the description and images or create them by yourself. The keywords are important because your listing will be indexed by Amazon depending on what keywords you choose. There are free and paid tools available to determine the best keywords.

A free tool is Google trends, which shows you the search frequency of a given keyword. Alternatively, you can use Merchant Words, which costs $30 a month to use. Merchant Words gives you data about the number of monthly searches that are occurring on Amazon for each keyword. You will want to find the most highly searched keywords and insert them into your title without making it seem obvious.

Once your listing is complete, the only remaining thing is the receipt of your inventory. Once your supplier ships the inventory, you can ask them to provide a tracking number. This tracking number can be inputted into your Amazon seller account, which will automatically track and update the status. On your seller account dashboard, the inventory will first show as zero. Once the inventory is delivered to the warehouse, there will be a slight delay (a few days) before all of the inventory changes from the "Receiving" status to the "Received" status. Once it is received, your products are officially live on Amazon.

Now, it is time to market your product and advertise it as much as possible. You will want to create a Facebook page and run Amazon Sponsored Ads. These ads will place you at the top of the search results and you will only be charged once someone clicks on your listing. These ads can be worth it if you are not spending too much and you are getting lots of sales through them.

The Product Launch stage is difficult. You will want to do a contest, or even giveaways of your products to create a buzz around your brand. When you begin to get lots of sales, Amazon will rank your product higher and higher until you reach the top of the search results for your main keywords without needing Amazon Sponsored Ads. However, it is still a good idea to keep running the ads because they will give you boost.

Once you begin to sell, your inventory will decrease as the days go by. It is important to keep track of your inventory so that you can order more at the right time from your supplier. As you begin to see your inventory fly in and out, you will realize that you have indeed launched a business online that is running almost automatically!

CHAPTER 3 - PHOTOGRAPHY

Photography is a great hobby for many and a good source of income for some. A lot of professional photographers claim that making money from photography is becoming harder by the day, but photographers that have come to appreciate the benefits of the Internet are reaping quite a bounty from their work. There are a lot of opportunities for photographers to make money online and I will show you a few methods.

Whatever your interest in photography; be it job or hobby, there are numerous ways you can make money from photography. All that is required is your camera, an online presence and some creativity.

Getting Started

It is advisable that you take a short online course on photography; that is if you are not already a photographer. There is in-depth knowledge that you must have in order to excel in this business. Online courses typically cover all of that and more. This will only make you a better photographer. Even if you already have experience in photography, it won't hurt to take a refresher course. It can help show you new ways of doing things and the new technology that is being used currently. There are a number of tutors offering photography courses on Udemy.

How to Become a Successful Photographer

The scope of this guide may not cover the techniques and practice of photography, but that's why I have encouraged you to take online courses.

Sell Stock Photography

You are already taking pictures; you have lots of portfolios filled with them. If this is the case, you can make good money selling stock photographs. Stock photographs are professional photographs of places, nature, events, people, public buildings or landmarks. This kind of photography has applications in articles, advert campaigns or anything really.

So, that photograph taken on your camping trip with Uncle Ben could just be worth some dollars. Selling stock photography is a great way to earn passive income because you would have taken the picture anyway. So, why not make money from it. There quite a number of platforms you can register with to upload your photographs for sale. The most popular are Shutter stock, Getty Image, Stocksy and Istock.

There is one thing to take note of before you register and start selling your photos. Take the time to read and understand the terms and conditions of the platform you are working with. Some of them prohibit you from licensing the same photographs with other platforms while others have limits on how much you must accrue from sales before any withdrawal can be made. Read carefully and when in doubt, do not hesitate to seek clarification from their respective customer support teams.

Sell Prints

If you are feeling a little adventurous, then I would ask that you sell prints. This will take you out of your comfort zone. With selling prints, you will be required to research what images sell the most. A simple search on Google could sort this out quickly. You may also be required to host your own photography website, where you will be charged with the responsibility of generating traffic to your website. Aside from implementing SEO strategies, you will need to make good use of social media to promote your website. There are platforms that you can use to outsource the tasks of transaction handling, shipping and printing. This allows you to focus on taking great pictures and promoting your website.

SmugMug and Pixieset have great platforms for new photographers who are looking to sell their photographs online.

This avenue is quite more profitable that uploading a stock photograph to major platforms. Here you can set your own pricing, terms and for the most part you are free to decide how you operate. The major task here is to invest in driving traffic to your website. You will need to blog while you're at it too, so you can create content for visitors outside of the images that you want to sell. This investment could be worthwhile when you start making at least a small income online.

CHAPTER 4 - EBOOK PUBLISHING

The Internet has changed the world we live in. Emails have replaced letters. Skype is now the new telephone exchange. We seldom rush down to the mall for purchases, but we can buy a house off the Internet. This is the world we live in today. Reading is gradually evolving just like the dissemination of information. Our whole lives have changed. This is the power of the Internet.

The Internet has opened a new vista of opportunity to make money and for businesses to expand into new markets.

Before now, say some 25 years back, in order to get access to books you needed to visit the library. There were giant publishers that ensured our cravings for knowledge were satisfied but somewhere along the line came the Internet to change the status quo. We now have Kindle and CreateSpace, ebooks have become a part of our vocabulary, many online businesses are starting up and the best part is that the promoters are just like you.

You can take on the world by publishing ebooks.

The big publishing houses may be closing down, but you've just opened up for business. The world is at your feet and ripe for the taking. Do you want to change your life and find financial freedom? Then this is just right for you.

Ebooks, as the name implies, are electronic books which can be downloaded online. Before now, writers would put together their manuscript and go shopping for publishers. Many times, good manuscripts found their place in the trashcan because the publishers didn't see any value in ithem. Several good writers have been frustrated by the cabalistic actions of publishers. But not anymore! Books can be written and published straight from your living room to the world.

Your ideas now truly have wings!

Getting Started

With ebooks, you don't have to worry about all the attendant challenges of traditional publishing. There is no need for expensive on paper or printing cost or having to deal with creating, storing, indexing or selling the hard copy. You are digital, you create your book, format it for Kindle and CreateSpace, and then you publish.

There are no publishing houses or administrative bureaucracy here. There are no forced lunches or smiling for the cameras (except if your book makes it to film). You are your own boss!

With ebooks, the scope of what you can write is wider. You can tailor your subject to any desired niche. You can create write-ups on travel, romance, fiction, technology or just about anything. As long as there is a market, you can write your heart out.

The Internet is filled with success stories of many self-published authors. Hugh Howey and Amanda Hocking are just a few of the names that have made it big as self-published authors. E.L. James, the author of 50 Shades of Grey, is also one of the names that has made it big through self publishing.

Where You Sell

Where to sell your book should be the least of your problems, the Internet has a lot of options for you. You can create your own website and sell your books on your platform, all it takes is just integrating a payment solution like PayPal onto it. Your customers will just get a download link to get the book after payment.

Another easy place to sell your ebooks is through Amazon. They are the largest marketplace for ebooks now with their Kindle (KDP) and CreateSpace. Amazon has the reach that gives your ebook the visibility it needs. Did you know that 38% of daily sales of ebooks on Amazon are from Self-published authors?

To get on a Kindle you just sign up, upload your ebook and get your sales.

Marketing Your Ebook

Ebook publishers have the advantage of using different channels to market their books. I suggest that you approach the marketing of your EBook from a range of angles. The best part is he Amazon has a program called KDP Select, in which you can use Amazon sponsored ads. These ads are great because they put your book at the top of the search results for your desired keyword.

Upon launching, it is advisable that you create buzz around the launch. Promote your book on your social media channels by providing links to your website so that interested parties can click on it and make a purchase Share your networks and encourage others to share too. To get users interested, you can offer a snap preview for readers. This serves as a teaser to encourage their purchasing of your books.

Do's and Don'ts

There are a few things you need to know when you make the decision to create an ebook. There are a few rules you have to keep in mind to avoid the pitfalls along the way. Making money from self-publishing is not so much of a smooth ride. What will set you apart are the strategies you apply to creating and marketing your ebook.

Below I have listed a few things to look out for and avoid:

1. Avoid stress.

2. Create an outline before you start writing.

3. Set a schedule of how you will work. You can't be working all day, create a schedule, and let it guide your work. The schedule is also to help you guide how you market your book and go through all the steps required to get your book to market.

4. Write about what you are confident about and only what you know.

5. Use easy language. Don't make your writing difficult to understand.

6. Proofread your manuscripts and correct all grammatical errors, misspellings, etc. Ask a friend to help double check for errors.

7. Create a professional look with your layout and cover. Invest in a good design; people really do judge a book by its cover.

Ebook publishing is for the discerning author. You don't have to have massive skill in writing, you can explore the option of using a ghostwriter to write while you publish it in your name. This is one of the ways some smart investors have chosen to take advantage of the e-publishing world.

CHAPTER 5 - PEER TO PEER LENDING

There has been a lot of buzz recently about this kind of investment stream. This is largely due to the consistently positive returns most operators have been seeing. Peer to peer lending, P2P lending, platform lending, or social lending, as it's sometimes called, is now a veritable source of earning passive income from a financial investment.

Reports have had it that while deposit certificates are returning annualized yields of 1.33% to 1.7% on money market and savings accounts still going at 0.54%, it is bound to create a buzz when you hear P2P lending returning annualized yields of between 5% and 15%, depending on the risk profile of the target investment.

What is P2P lending and how is it able to generate so much revenue? This is the same question on the lips of some of the smartest investors looking to take advantage of the business tide. I have gone on to try it myself and I will detail a step-by-step guide on how to invest in P2P lending platforms, what you need to look out for, as well as the risk factors and how to mitigate them.

This investment is very profitable. Aside from the monetary benefits you derive as an investor, it is safe to assume that you are also encouraged by the desire to do some good. Peer-to-peer lending uses the principle of crowdsourcing. The platform pools together lenders looking for individuals or businesses to finance at a rate that is way above the market rate, and there are no hassles of paperwork.

Peer to peer lending is a social gathering of individuals who pull resources together to finance loans for individuals or small businesses outside the traditional financial system. Let us assume that a registered member (John) of XYZ social lending platform needs $2,000 to start-up his small business. He can request for such a business from the platform. The moderators assess his eligibility and rate his credit worthiness after which, if found good enough for the business, his application gets a nod for bidding by potential investors. Investors decide on how much they want to invest at all times. Of the $2,000 request, he could have as much as 20 people pool the resources for him or even one person offer the loan to him. All of these are managed by the moderators of the platform.

The money pooled by the individuals represents a percentage investment in the facility. For instance, John gets the loan at 25%, the lending platform aggregates the sum and pays out an amount monthly to the investors according to their invested amounts.

These platforms like Lending Club (one of the biggest social lending platforms on the Internet) handle all transactions and communications between you, the investor and the one seeking the loan. You may not handle the process, but you have a choice of deciding your risk exposure.

Getting Started

To start investing in P2P, it is important to have an objective. There is a need here to apply a specific strategy which is born out of your objectives. Why do you want to invest in P2P? Does the investment profile fit your personality? How much are you looking to invest? And how do you want to allocate your investment?

Because the choice of what to invest in lies solely in your palms, you have to develop and apply a strategy. You could try to give loans out only to small businesses because of the security associated with such loans, or your focus could be on people in certain kinds of employment. Whatever your strategy, research and stick with it. You may have to fine tune it as you go along, but it is important that you stick with it. Do not sway.

Social Lending Platforms

These are the platform on which lending and borrowing take place. This platform mirrors your social network and it brings together people of like minds looking to invest. Investment in these platforms takes the form of committing to providing a loan to any of the many eligible applicants on the platform. There are a few leading platforms on the Internet. Let us look at their facts and figures to see if it's convincing enough to encourage you to consider this investment asset.

Lending Club: This is currently the biggest and the most popular social lending platform. They started back in 2007 and since then, they have been providing investors and borrowers alike a stable business model for all to thrive.

There are two loan categories: individuals and businesses. Individuals are offered facilities between $1,000 - $35,000, and businesses between $15,000 and $300,000. They properly vet borrowers and classify them into grades according to their credit score. The grading is also the determinate to how much money they can request.

For investors, a minimum investment of $1,000 is required to be listed on Lending Club. Interest rates range from the type of loans you opt to invest in and the amount you put up.

Prosper Loans: They started out in 2006. Unlike Lending Club, they only provide loans to individuals. Their loan amount ranges from $2,000 - $35,000.

The minimum investment with Prosper is $25. With just $25, you can start offering loans to borrowers. Prosper is a good start for those trying out P2P for the first time without having to risk large initial capital. You can create and test strategies and once you get a hang of them, you can then raise your investment or move to a larger platform.

Upstart: They have just recently launched. They came on stream in 2014 and in that time have been able to raise over $300 million in loans. Their target audience includes young professionals, recent graduates and startups. The loan term is fixed for 4 – 5 years and interest rates are between 4% and 26%. The minimum investment with Upstart is $100.

Upstart is the game changer here. Where other platforms charge an origination fee to the lender's account, Upstart does so to the borrower. They also bear the risk of any default should it occur (mind you, they have the best repayment rates 94%). You get your money back paid in full by Upstart. With this platform you don't get to pick your borrower, you instead invest in a grade.

Benefits of Social Lending

This is an inexpensive way to set up a loan shark. Ideally, if you were to invest in a loan shark business, you would have to take into consideration a lot of factors, from permits to office, stationery, advertising, investing in debt collection, etc. And you would deal solely with defaults which in some cases could destroy your business. With social lending, you also have that capacity. You don't have to allocate a large sum of your investment, as a small sum can give you an aggregated advantage as if you had invested a large amount. Your investment is fairly safe since the moderators tend to conduct proper background and credit rating checks to further guarantee the security of your investment.

They provide quick and easy facilities for borrowers usually over the Internet, and without the hassles of paperwork.

For the investor, with startups like Upstart, this is a safe and inexpensive way to earn regular income for your investment.

Risk

The high yield is a tradeoff for risk. This is not to say that the process or investment is a cesspit where money can just vanish but your exposure is way higher here than with traditional investment assets. The first risk to consider is default.

Default: P2P loan platforms are largely non-collateralized loan facilities, they are similar in that way to credit card advances. With a non-collateralized facility comes the high risk of default. In this case here, the consequence the borrower incurs is a negative on his credit score and the attendant charges on his loan. There is no car or house to repossess.

Be mindful and make sure that the promised return is worth the inherent risk. However, reports published by Lending Club showed defaults were very minimal and also statistical financial reports have shown lower rates of defaults on unsecured loans than their secure counterparts.

Lack of Government Backing: The Federal Deposit Insurance Corporation ensures and guarantees investors funds in deposit certificates and treasury bills but that is not the case with P2P lending. The investment is not insured and you stand the risk of losing both capital and and any gains.

Liquidity Risk: Unlike stocks and bonds, you can't just opt out of the blue and liquidate your investment in P2P. Because of the nature of the investment, you may have to wait out the tenure.

Mitigating the Risk

There are several ways you can minimize your risk exposure and still benefit from the high yield profile of P2P. There are a few strategies I will show you that will help you decide on the best course of action to take.

Diversification: it is advised that rather than place a lump sum investment in a single loan, it will be smart to place smaller sums on multiple loans so in case one should default, you don't lose all your money and interest.

Strategy: Develop a strategy and hedge against default. One such way to do this is to spread your investments across different platforms. Leverage the individuality of the Lending Club and hedge with Upstart. It may sound a little complex but in simple terms, the Lending Club allows you to pick your investments, which in turn gives you a greater perspective on how your money should be used. You can maximize your returns here. Upstart can be used to hedge against loss on the Lending Club since Upstart takes full responsibility of defaults.

This business would require further study, and I advise that you start out with Prosper to learn the ropes. After that you can move on to the others. This is one fine way of making money. Take advantage of this opportunity.

CHAPTER 6 - VIDEOGRAPHY

Videography, like photography, is a great hobby for many and a good source of income. A lot of professional videographers are now able to make more money due to the Internet and social media. Businesses looking to place adverts on social media platforms are turning to videographers to shoot a compelling clip that advertises their business. There are a lot of opportunities for videographers to make money online and I will be showing you a few of them.

No matter if you pick up the camera as a hobby or if you are a professional, there are numerous ways you can make money from your craft. All that is required is your camera, an online presence, creativity and promotion.

Getting Started

To derive maximum benefit from this business, it is advisable that you take a short online course on videography and video editing; that is if you are not actively creating videos as of now or you know next to nothing about the craft.

There is special knowledge you must have if you are to succeed in this business, some of which includes lighting, camera angles, focus, editing, etc. Online courses will cover all of that and more. There are new technologies, animated effects, editing, and proofing. You can get training from any online course marketplace.

How to Make Money

In this guide, I will be showing you opportunities you can take advantage of in your business. Below are just a few ways to monetize videos.

Sell Stock Videos

Stock videos are professional videos of places, nature, events, people, public buildings or landmarks. This kind of video, depending on its quality and subject, can have applications in documentaries, advertising campaigns, or any other form of commercial purpose. There are quite a number of platforms you can register with to upload your videos for sale. The most popular ones are Getty Image, Stocksy and Istock.

Promote on YouTube

Uploading your video to YouTube is a great way to make money that will also help to promote your craft. If you are a nature lover, you can create a video journal documenting your exploits on YouTube, and gain subscribers from fellow enthusiasts. Great partnerships have been known to form from these sites. You never know, you could possibly find your video on National Geographic.

Make Promotional Videos

There are a lot of businesses looking for videographers to help create them professional videos for promotional purposes. With your experience and expertise, you can excel at such jobs. You could also create videos for ceremonies such as weddings and graduations.

One other way you can monetize your skill is to shoot videos for musicians, local bands and theatrical plays. You can even have a partner write screenplays while you shoot them. The videos can be uploaded to YouTube or sold to television channels.

One of the major social networks you can utilize to promote your work and website is Instagram. It is also a fertile ground for collaboration. As you grow your social media following, look out for companies you can collaborate with. One aspect of promotion that must not be overlooked is using SEO to improve your ranking. On your website, include the right keywords in your titles and implement meta-tagging. The key is to find the right keywords that would display your site when clients search Google for photographers or anything relating to photography.

Affiliate Marketing

One fun way to make money from your already growing popularity is affiliate marketing. You are already on your way to gaining those one million followers, so why not utilize your growing followership to become an affiliate for some products. The process is easy. You would only be required to sign up online, and once approved, you can start posting links alongside the content that brings the followers back. Companies like Amazon Associates have great affiliate programs that you can take advantage of.

Freelancing

Freelancing is another great way to make money as a videographer. Platforms like Upwork and Fiverr provide you with a base to market your works to customers who need it. If these sites don't fulfill that need, you can try videography specific platforms like Thumbtack and Video To Order. The process of getting jobs there is quite straight forward, just place bids for listed offers and if you win the bid, you get the job. Simple!

Teach

This is one way you can earn more money. There are a couple of people interested in videography but do not know where to start. You can share what you know with them and get paid. There are several ways to do this. You can create an online course for aspiring videographers or create a YouTube series that focuses videography basics.

Online Video Editor

Your knowledge in video editing is also a marketable skill. Just as you use it to better your craft, you can also offer it as a service on your website. Interested clients can upload their videos to your website and you can help them by editing for a fee.

CHAPTER 7 - DOMAIN FLIPPING

Domain flipping is one of the oldest ways of making money on the Internet. Since the dot com era, lots of savvy Internet entrepreneurs have cashed in on the business of domain flipping. Understanding how domain flipping works is quite easy. It is the understanding of how the market works that gets you the real money.

Buying a domain at a low price doesn't mean you will sell it for a higher price. You might fail at it if things are not laid out well. The important thing to consider when going into this business is the market. How do you market your domain?

Before we proceed, allow me to show you just how profitable it is to flip domains. There have been major milestones surpassed in domain flipping. Some domains have sold for over $30,000,000. The website Marijuana.com sold for $8,888,888 in 2011 on heels of the mainstream cannabis adoption. But that's not all. There are regular domain auctions on www.flippa.com, an online website and domain auction platform.

Here is a list of some of the domains that have attracted prices in the millions of dollars.

1.   Medicare.com 2014 - $4.8 million

2.   Candy.com 2009 - $3 million

3.   Insure.com 2009 - $16 million

4.   Fund.com 2008 - $9.99 million

5.   mi.com 2014 - $3.6 million

These are just a few. There are some more sites out there that have this same earning potential. If the millions sound too far out of reach, you can always look out for some small valued sites worth a couple thousands of dollars.

Getting Started

Over 300,000 domains are being registered daily and this comes to about 109,500,000 registered domains a year. Looking at these numbers tells you that there is a huge market for domain flipping.

This is the catch: Most of the domains registered yearly don't get to live past their first year. Often times, once they expire they are abandoned.

This is the business: These expired domains can be bought by you for pennies on the dollar and then sold for hundreds if not thousands of dollars. Because new businesses are always looking for popular domains, you can cash in on this and make some good money for yourself. Your responsibility is to find good domains, make them yours for cheap and then sell to eager buyers.

Finding the Right Domain

Finding the right domain to purchase for flipping is essential to your success in this business. There are a few factors to consider when investing here. I shall provide the best five factors to consider and the tools to help you make a successful decision. It is important that you know how to judge the quality of a domain and its value.

These are some of the factors to consider when getting your domains:

Consider DOT COM (.com) Domains Only: You should invest only in .COM domains. This is an ideal domain for businesses. Most customers assume the domain to be a .com when told the web address. This is also the domain extension with the highest resale value. Over 50% of all domains sold are .com extensions. You can even leverage your name by purchasing other link extensions and link them to your .com extension.

Pick an Easy Name: The name should be easy to remember and pronounce. Most people have a better affinity with 2 – 3 syllable domains, although this is not the norm and all I am saying is avoid unnecessarily long names, like names with hyphens or numbers. Keep it short and simple.

Look out for Branding: You will have to be a little creative here. Names that sound like brands sell faster and attract more value. For instance; consider a name like cookieJar.com, this name sounds brandable. This is not difficult to do, just think about it a little and it will come to you. Businesses are looking to pay thousands for names that sync with their brand. Sometimes it is the domain name that gives them an idea of what to call their business.

Keywords Only: This involves finding names that match specific niches. Someone setting up a medical business would want something along the lines of medicine. Domain names that are keywords, or are keyword related, sell faster and have good value.

The Right Value of the Domain: This is the most critical point in finding the right domain. If you make a mistake here, you could lose a lot of money. The value of a domain lies in the number of its backlinks, its relevance and quality. The more backlinks a domain has the more powerful and valuable it becomes. The position of the backlinks is also important as backlinks within the content matters more. There several tools online that will determine this, including the Moz site explorer.

When purchasing domains, make sure that the domains are of good quality, and although the earning potential may be huge, you can still get a loss sometimes if you don't apply the right strategies. Domains can be purchased from various domain registration platforms like www.godaddy.com.

CHAPTER 8 - SOCIAL MEDIA MANAGER

Businesses have reasoned social media to be a viable marketing tool. They have deployed marketing strategies but most of the time, these strategies have not always made their desired mark, and this is due in part to poor planning and poor execution of such strategies. Social media is a different playing field. Brands that want to take advantage of the enormous market must be ready to adopt new strategies as the traditional marketing strategies have failed woefully on these spaces. Well, there is no one else to turn to but the social media manager.

Social media management is a confluence of tasks aimed at promoting a particular business or brand on social media. The tasks include but are not limited to content marketing, public relations, customer service, social media strategies, and community growth and management.

Who is a Social Media Manager?

A social media manager is that tech savvy, technology-loving, sometimes smooth-talking strategist that helps businesses market themselves through various methods on social media. The services offered by social media managers include:

1. Social media account setup

2. Social media management strategy

3. Social media audits

4. Content marketing

5. Social media advertising

The social media manager is expected to build a strategy around the social media marketing objective of his client. There are no specific skills required but going by the job requirements, a social media manager should be a good reader, writer, communicator, and he or she should understand and follow trends. The social media manager should be a deadline-conscious individual with great customer service skills.

How Much Do Social Media Managers Earn

The earning opportunities here are diverse. It depends on the client, your strategy for the client, and what works best for you. Some clients offer a fixed payment for a certain range of services while others will be willing to pay per hour. Irrespective of whatever option, the job of a social media manager is very lucrative. The pay is good as some managers are earning as much as $200 per hour. Your rates will be determined by your skill, the task at hand, and your experience. Someone who has worked for five years with big brands will command a higher rate than someone who is just starting out.

How to be Successful at Social Media Management

There are certain practices that put you in great standing as a social media manager. These are not the only things you may require but they are good enough to get you going as a successful social media manager.

Develop a Strategy: Most successful social media managers have preset strategies to pitch to their clients. Develop strategies, test these strategies under various scenarios on your profile and document the result.

This is a good way to show the client that you have what it

takes to undertake the task. Show the client that you are versatile and can adapt to different trends and scenarios. These will also help you develop service packages based on the options you have tested.

Advertise Your Platform: It is only good business practice that dictates you to have a website. This is where visitors can reach you. Here they get to know more about you, what you are offering and the price. Your website is a window to better knowing who you are and what you stand for.

You don't have to go for something overly elaborate, a good WordPress website will do just fine.

Find Work

After you have perfected your strategies, built a good following on social media, and after you have been able to create a great website, then we should move on to finding work.

Sourcing for clients is no menial task. You may have to leverage your offline networks to get your first one, but should that be unavailable you can try out these ideas:

Conferences and Meetups: Look out for conferences around your local area, especially those that are related to your desired niche. Do not neglect the offer of a lunch or coffee over the break. These are important times you can pitch your service to prospective clients.

Referrals: Ask for referrals from friends and colleagues. Make your immediate network your first place of searching. If you have also been practicing test strategies on your profile, it is possible a few people have noticed. Do not be afraid to ask for referrals. You never know, they may not even be thinking about it but know someone who needs your service.

Guest Posting: Never turn down an opportunity to share your knowledge and expertise on blogs or newsletters. This is one great way to let prospective clients in on your service offerings.

Create a Schedule

Once your efforts at finding work start to pay off, it is important that you create a schedule since things can quickly get out of hand, especially if you are working with multiple clients. Create a plan that works for you but make sure that it reflect the goals of your clients. Let your strategy function effectively under whatever schedule you create. One great way you can get help with scheduling is online. Look out for social media managers that are excelling and replicate their strategy.

There are quite a number of tools that can help you with scheduling; some even offer reports and moderation capacities as added features. The best tool for me is HootSuite.

HootSuite: This is the scheduler in my opinion. It offers the best features and functionality. It is affordable and has features that monitor conversations and mentions.

Feedback is quite crucial in social media management. It is feedback that will determine which strategy is working and which is not. It also gives your clients the opportunity to evaluate their investment. Ensure that your tools produce adequate and proper reporting. It will make you a better professional.

Continuing Education: This is very crucial. As you grow, you will have to continue investing in education. There is a lot to learn. Besides tools that facilitate some of your responsibilities, there is other knowledge that you will need to acquire as you move forward. That knowledge should include graphics, advertising and SEO.

Graphics: Knowledge in graphics will go a long way in helping your craft. Most people are drawn more to visuals than text. The ability to share your idea in the form of images, graphs or illustrated art is a big plus because it allows for greater user engagement.

SEO: Understanding and the ability to implement SEO strategies is really important for your brand. Learn the various methods to implementing SEO, the importance of tags and keywords, and how to use them for the maximum benefit to your client. Learn optimization for social media networks like Facebook and Pinterest.

Advertisement: Learn how to invest in targeted advertising and promotion. There are lots of courses on the Internet that offer free training on this, take advantage of them to better implement the best promotion strategy for your brand.

CHAPTER 9 - FOREX TRADING

Before we begin, I must make this very clear: The trade on commodities, Forex, options, and futures are very volatile investments and there is a high probability that you can lose all your money.

Forex trading is also known as foreign currency exchange trading, and it is the trade of international currencies. The prices of currencies fluctuate over time and as a Forex trader, it is your responsibility to look out for trends that foretell the direction in which a particular currency will fluctuate.

Currencies are like any other commodities in the world, their value is also affected by market forces, and thus the currency either rises in value (Bullish) or loses some of its value

(Bearish).

The global online Forex market is the largest financial trading market in the world. There is conflicting data as to exactly how large the market is, but there is one common denominator and that is that the market has a daily trading volume in the trillions of dollars. The market is a 24 hour, 7 days a week market that attracts traders from all over. It is quite easy to trade Forex which is exactly why people do this. Aside from the ease of setting up an account, the Forex market offers significant leverage, low startup cost, opportunities to practice strategies before taking the plunge, and a range of investment options. You don't have to worry about driving traffic here nor do you consider the impact of SEO/SEM, but you must be ready invest a lot of time in education (which is absolutely free by the way) and the practice of new techniques.

Rule of Thumb: Forex is not for everyone, so it is important that you determine if you have the right temperament and mindset required to successfully trade Forex.

Summary

Forex, simply put, is the exchange of currencies. The currency in use in the US is the dollar ($), the currency in use in Germany is the Euro (€). You would have to exchange your dollars for euros when you get to Germany because with your dollars, you can't make purchases. One important thing to consider when exchanging your dollars for euros is that the rates are subject to fluctuations. You could get a higher rate today than what was exchanged for on the previous day.

If that is understood, let us then consider this same practice of exchange is moved onto the online world and ordinary people engage in the exchange with a motive of profiting from the fluctuations. This is online Forex trading. You invest in a particular currency pair exchange (USD/EUR, USD/GBP or GBP/EUR etc.) with the motive to profit from the rise in the value of one currency over its pair.

The beauty of this kind of trade is the ease at which it occurs. You can trade from your living room, kitchen counter, patio, office or from anywhere else. All that is required is an Internet enabled mobile device or computer, an account with a broker, and your first investment.

CHAPTER 10 - ONLINE ECOMMERCE STORE

There has never been a better time to start an online ecommerce business than now. The ever-growing reliance on online stores for purchases has made this amazing business one to explore. With the growing number of buyers turning to online stores, the future of ecommerce looks very good.

Ecommerce businesses come in various sizes and scopes. From the giants like Amazon and Shopify to the small businesses looking to carve a niche and reach online, the opportunities are endless. Online buyers have been increasing. As of 2016, it is estimated that there are over 1.5 billion online buyers and the number will continue to rise as more people embrace the digital space.

Ecommerce platforms come in two distinct types. The first is an offshoot of an already existing business. Here, you create an online platform where customers can purchase your product. These products could range from physical products like health and skin care products to digital products such as ebooks, recipes and video tutorials.

The second module is where you have a platform that is developed for small businesses who would want to sell online. Small businesses can create and operate their own stalls on your platform while you advertise and market on their behalf. This module would require significant capital as it is akin to what the likes of Amazon are currently doing. The primary motivation of setting up and launching a platform where designers, entrepreneurs, and other creative artists can sell their merchandises is more attainable now than ever before.

"With Ecommerce, you have to build credibility and trust

because you are not visible to your audience/customers, it is expected that they would be skeptical," says Roxanne King, the owner of Holistic Mama, which is a natural skin care and beauty products manufacturer with a long running and successful Ecommerce site.

Before we start out on building trust, let's take a look at what is required to set up, launch and maintain an Ecommerce platform.

Setting Up

1.   One of the keys to a successful startup of any business is to create a marketing buzz; this is no different for an Ecommerce business. The idea here is to make good use of your social network. You could create a buzz about your entry into the market and have your contacts share it. You could create a hashtag on twitter and aim at making it trend, whatever you do, just make sure you are noticed.

2.   Decide on the kind of Ecommerce platform you want to operate. Are you going to be creating a product and selling it on the platform as another marketing and product promotion channel or will you be providing a platform for small businesses to advertise and pursue sales? It is important that you define your platform and business model first.

3.   Pick a name. There is so much in a name. Find a name that resonates with the ideas of your business, it must be catchy, 3 syllables at most and easy to pronounce. It is around this you will build your brand identity. Whatever name you pick, make sure that its domain is available.

4.   Finally, decide on the right service to design your Ecommerce business. There are several services available, let's take a look at the offerings of the big 4: Woo Commerce,

Shopify, Magento and SquareSpace. All of them with the exception of SquareSpace are available as WordPress plugins to add to your existing website. With SquareSpace, you can create a new website from scratch.

Woo Commerce

Woo Commerce is free to download. This plugin has free themes for use but you can purchase premium themes and extensions starting at $39 and $249 respectively. Some technical knowledge is required.

Magento

This is an open-source framework. This platform requires a good working knowledge of how to code web platforms. You can get the Community Edition for free or the much more complex Enterprise solution at $18,000 a year.

SquareSpace Commerce

This is an all-in-one-solution that comes with two levels—Basic at $30/month and the Advanced level at $80/month. There is no technological knowledge required for this service as it is a one-click service.

Shopify

It is quite easy to use and integrate and there are four plans on offer with this service. The first is the Lite Plan ($9/month) and the second option is the Unlimited ($179/month) Plan. It would be a good idea to start with the Lite Plan and you can always upgrade toe the Unlimited Plan later as your business grows.

Launch

After you have made a choice of the type of platform you hope to develop and the service you intend to use, you should get it up and running. The point here is to get experience as fast as you can. Lots of people do not launch as soon as they can because they are perfectionists. A lot of the learning and improving things will be done on the fly, as that is part of the ecommerce business.

You can hire influencers to get the word out, either on radio, social media and even on TV. There are some freelancers on Fiverr.com that will promote your business on radio for a small fee. I would recommend that you search for these types of services as they can really help you get off the ground.

Maintain

Irrespective of the service, plan or platform builder you choose, you have to put in work to maintain your platform and have it running smoothly. Associated fees such as transaction fees and merchant fees now form the bulk of your overhead. It will do you well to invest in content management and marketing apps to provide better functionality. These apps sell pop ups, which help to further drive sales.

Further investment in email marketing and search engine optimization (SEO) is also advised. You should integrate customer service and tools to manage customer relationship as part of your store-building exercise. It is advised that you have active phone and email support in order to both help existing customers and convert new visitors into loyal customers.

Make Successful

The most important step in making your store successful will be to have a unique brand. There are lots of branding specialist out there that you can hire if you don't want to do this on your own. The look and reputation of your brand will grow slowly, but it is your job to ensure that there is very limited or no negativity regarding your brand among the public.

If your intention is to create the first type of ecommerce store mentioned above, take the initiative to also rely on larger platforms for growth. Sell through a larger outlet like Amazon; it gives your products the needed visibility and also tests your popularity on a larger scale. You are most likely to get repeat customers from these platforms because they have built trust with their customers. Maintaining your own vision is paramount to building a successful Ecommerce platform but do not neglect other platforms with brand names that can help the growth of your store. There may be a need to collaborate, so don't turn down that opportunity.

Postscript

There are a lot of benefits in setting up a business such as this one. The opportunity for growth and profitability depends on your mindset and what kind of strategies you employ. I can't exactly tell you how much money you can make but look around you, there are lots of success stories from Amazon to Etsy to Holistic Mama, each of them are successes in their own right. They all had to put in work and understand the business environment they chose to operate in.

The investment for an online business is much lower than a traditional one. There are no heavy overhead charges, shipping can be taken care of by a third party drop shipping agency and you are even open 24/7. It is so much easier and less costly to expand operations if the need arises. But like all businesses, customer retention is the key to success. Invest in programs and content that would help retain your customers. Build a mobile-friendly website or design a mobile app. This will be a definite bonus because more people are accessing platforms through mobile apps and this number is expected to continue to rise. Treat your ecommerce business like you would treat any other offline business, obtain permits where necessary and always pay your taxes. The last thing you want is trouble from the taxman.

CHAPTER 11 - 3D PRINTING

Just run a search on the Internet for 3D printing, or how to make money from 3D printing, and you'll be amazed at the ton of resources that hit you. Authority blogs like Livewire and Mashable have covered topics and created lists on the subject.

Let's begin by understanding what 3D printing is about. Most people who have never seen 3D printing before refer to the process as magic. The gradual coming to form of each composite layer and the unveiling of the final product is a wonder to behold. Many enthusiasts have claimed to experience a cathartic feeling at the end of the process.

My concern here though is how you can profit from this fast growing technology. The journey to making money from 3D printing is going to be one to remember. It has allowed others to reach heights of emotional exuberance, with technology breaks occurring daily. The technology is being used to change the lives of veterans who lost limbs on their tour of duty and automobile businesses that are exploring concepts made through 3D printing. There are lots of details to hash out, including selecting the right type of printer, the tools to acquire and gaining access to printers without spending so much.

3D Printing has been defined as an additive manufacturing process that creates a physical object from a digital image. This is more like you design something on your computer, run it through the 3D printing software, and Voila! The physical object is printed. And the beautiful thing about the technology is that you can print using different materials.

Getting Started

To start out with 3D printing, you need to understand a bit more about the technology, what it offers, what its limits are and what skills you need to have before going down this road.

3D printing has been around for a long time, but before 2009 it was primarily used for industrial and research purposes. In 2009, commercialization of the process began following the expiration of the FDM patent. This allowed printers that were sold for up to $200,000 to be mass produced and sold for less than $2,000. Thus, the rave was born.

The various technologies that exist for 3D printing are FDM, SLA/DLP, SLS, Material Jetting, Binder Jetting, and Metal Printing. Each technology has its own preferred material. I won't be delving too deep into that because that's a lot of technical stuff but I will tell you this: the main materials that are used for 3D printing include paper, gypsum, sand, plastic and metal.

Create a Design

To start with 3D printing, you have to have a 3-dimensional design of what you want printed. Knowledge of design using any of the CAD software available on the market is required. Although you can have a CAD professional make designs for you, you could also learn the software on your own and make your designs. The idea behind this is to help you better express your creativity. Software like Autodesk tinkerCAD, Autodesk 123D design, Blender and Sketchup are available for free on the Internet.

Better yet, find something three dimensional you like on the Internet. There are a lot of content platforms offering free and paid designs that can be printed in 3D.

Find a Printer

There are different ways to go about this. You can find a service online where you pay for the service or you purchase your own printer. Since you are looking to make money from it, I would suggest an investment in your own printer.

There are a couple of advantages using the different methods. For starters, with an online service, you don't have to make the first large investment in a printer, you have options of printing using a variety of materials, and you have access to the latest technologies. While it may seem laudable, you are also limited to experimenting with 3D printing unlike if you had a printer of your own. You get to print often and experiment with designs.

If you go with owning a printer, you would have to consider the technology, cost, space, what you intend on printing, and the type of material you would be printing with. Most FDM printers are low cost (under $2,000) and effective for printing using plastic and nylon. They don't do too well with intricate designs however. So decide on the kind of objects you want to print, your proposed capital investment, and the space that will be occupied by your ideal printer.

Make Money

Once you have cleared the hurdle of finding a printer, whether it's an investment in a printer or a printing service, the next point is to monetize your business. There are several ways you can make money from 3D printing. There are a few below:

Create and Sell Designs: One of the ways to make money from 3D printing is to create unique designs and sell them. On eBay and Etsy, you can sell uniquely designed phone docks, flower vases, or small pieces of art. You can also browse content providers for inspiration. Blender has an e-shop that sells colorful and creative designs for various purposes.

Offer 3D Printing Services: This is mostly dependent on the amount you have available to invest in a printer. When choosing this path, it is important to consider the cost, versatility of the printer and its size. You would also need to connect to a network. This helps you jump on the radar of those who would want your services. 3D hubs are currently the largest networks that you will definitely want to explore.

Create a Website: You can create a website and have users sign up so that they can create their designs, or you can print them instead. Your platform should be interactive and engaging. You could also create a store for your already printed items and have them ready for sale.

Design Prototypes: This is applicable to the manufacturing, fashion, IT, engineering and design industries. At one point or another, there is a need to make a prototype or a model for your projects. Collaborate with designers and offer your services to print prototypes, models and physical simulations for them.

Teach. You can take advantage of all that experience you have learned and earn some money by teaching a budding enthusiast about the technology and how they can take advantage of it. There are people who are interested and would need you to help guide them.

These are just some of the few ways you can start a 3D printing service and profit from this amazing technology. Although the products have a few drawbacks that are related to durability and tensile strength, the industry is rapidly improving and seeking new ways to tackle these challenges. This is one of the futuristic businesses where you can make money and still fulfill a passion. For me, I get "wowed" by it daily and I am sure you will feel the same way.

CHAPTER 12 - GRAPHIC DESIGN

Online graphic design has been around for quite a while, but it is gradually gaining momentum with an influx of people now offering their services online. Graphic design is very popular these days, and as more people learn graphic design the question on their mind is, "What jobs are available?"

First off, not just anyone can make money online as a graphic designer. It goes way beyond having great skills and mastering the art of design. To make money online, you need to understand the market and its needs. With graphic design, you will definitely need an edge to succeed. One such edge is expanding your skill set so you can take on larger design projects.

Getting Started

The quickest way a graphic designer can earn money consistently online is by designing and creating logos, as well as ad designs. This sort of work is always available for graphic designers since most businesses require these services at one point or another.

How to Make Money From Graphic Design

Freelance Platforms

One of the best places to make money online as a graphics designer is to become a freelancer. A lot of freelance platforms exist where clients are seeking freelance graphics designers.

It is advisable that you start out small. Do not price yourself too high, I know that you may want to feel discouraged with some of the amounts being offered but do not be dismayed. Accept offers, build your portfolio, and when you have been able to gather up a number of positive ratings, and have built a good standing for yourself, you can then gradually increase your fees.

The beauty of these platforms is that you set your work hours. You're in charge of your time and work schedule. Most of the jobs will be logos, brochure designs, flyers and book covers. The best freelance platforms online for the aspiring graphic designers include Fiverr, Upwork, 99 Designs and 48 Hours Logo.

Having Your Own Website

One of the really great ways you can also excel online as a graphics designer is by having your own website. This would serve as your base of operations and a place to host all your content. There are a number of ways you can approach this. You can have your website set up to sell your services as a graphics designer, or you can just have it as a gallery showing your works with your contact details and links to your freelance accounts on various freelance platforms.

The best way I suggest you achieve this is to create a blog. It is very easy and you don't have to the break the bank in order to achieve this. You can have them fully optimized, mobile friendly, and you can infuse keywords and meta tags. This will allow you to take great advantage of your platform as you can earn from Google Ad Sense, Affiliate Marketing, or personal display ads.

The opportunities when you have your website are great, but it can also cause you to become hidden, unlike the freelance platforms that already attract a lot of people who may be seeking your services. I would suggest that you do not rely only on your website or blog, but instead use it as a link to show your portfolio while also taking advantage of the many jobs offers that exist on the freelance platforms.

Promote and Advertise

After putting things in place, you need to advertise and be seen. With freelance websites, you can get noticed and get sales without driving any traffic to yourself. People are already in the know of the services offered on those platforms. The real job on the platform is to deliver good and creative jobs when your bid is accepted. The more positive reviews you get, the better your profile will become, and in no time you'll start getting generic offers without having to bid for them. This is not to say that you cannot promote your gigs on your social networks or other forums where people would likely be looking for your service.

Another great way to ensure you turn up on generic search engines is to implement SEO. This is referred to as a series of actions taken to ensure that your website or blog get seen on generic web searches. The important thing to note here is keywords. Research keywords about designs you create and infuse those keywords into your titles, meta tags, and content you create for your website or blog.

The content you create could be in the form of articles written on a subject concerning design. You don't have to be a great writer to achieve this. There are others like you on freelance platforms that will, for a small fee, help you create content for your website. You get to decide on what you want to be created. Instagram is a great place to showcase your art so you definitely want to be using it.

Texture Packs

This is something I discovered that is great for marketing.

Although it may sound silly at first, you should consider how they are used in popular games. Design texture packs for high profile games like Minecraft, and place them in your advertisements. They will sell your services better and give you a boost in advertising.

CHAPTER 13 - VLOGGING

Video blogs, popularly called vlogs, are no longer simple hobbies or diversions for entertainment purposes. Vlogging is the act of publishing videos on video publishing platforms such as YouTube. They have become one of the many ways people are making money online, to the extent where some are even making millions of dollars!

How Much do Vloggers Earn?

In this business, there are those who have made it real big. They command an impressive followership and have been able to convert that followership to 6 and 7 figure incomes. We can't talk about video blogging without mentioning the likes of PewDiePie; the king of vlogging, he made over $15 million in 2016 alone and commands an impressive 54 million YouTube subscribers.

Besides PewDiePie, there are other giants like HolaSoyGerman, who earns over $5 million yearly by vlogging about comedy, music and video games. There is Evans Fong, a 24 year old Canadian who vlogs while playing video games and Yuya, who is a 23 year old beauty vlogger from Mexico.

Realistically, making money in the millions from vlogging is not going to be an easy task, but the good news is you can still make enough to take care of some bills. You only need to invest 3 – 5 hours weekly, a good camera, a video editor, some business skills, this guide and a bang idea! Hitting a $1000 a month with a Vlog is not that far-fetched for someone starting out. The key is to keep it simple.

Getting Started

Building your vlog's reputation and viewership to the level

where you are making serious money from Google AdSense will definitely take some time and effort, but you can explore other streams of revenue from your vlog channel. To better understand the vlog ecosystem, let us consider Olga Kay.

Sometime in 2014, the NY Times featured an article on Olga Kay; she is a vlogger with several channels on YouTube to her credit. She says that she lives off vlogging; she earns $100,000 to $300,000 yearly from Google AdSense. She makes about 20 video posts a week. She has been able to grow her subscriber base to over 1 million and is leveraging on this number to further monetize her vlog.

She has marketed herself and vlog to advertisers that now pay $75 CPR if she shows certain products in her video. Ford gifted her with a car with 1 year of free gas, on the condition that she must show the car in a video at least once a month. She just opened her own socks store and she's sending lots of viewers in L.A. to buy them.

Making lots of money from Vlogging does require great business sense and a willingness to go above and beyond. It all comes down to your ability to diversify and scale.

Moving on, the earning potential of YouTube Partners is determined by a number of factors, one of which is the type of ads that can be displayed on their videos. Each video uploaded has a target audience and displayed ads must be relevant to that audience; it has to be something they are interested in and if they are interested in your blog, the ads should be somehow relevant to your content.

Some niches offer more bucks per ad than others. The amount you get paid will also depend on your viewers' predisposition. In all, the CPM for many of the channels varies around $0.30

and $2.50. The people on Youtube earn a little higher than $2.00 per thousand views, while only a fraction earn more than $3.00 per thousand views.

From the analysis we just made, you can see that to make money relying only on Google AdSense may not really be a great business strategy. But what we learn from PewDiePie and Olga Kay is that the trick to making really good money from vlogging is to use your platform as a content marketing tool. Vloggers either sell their own products or those of their affiliates through their videos.

There are a lot of affiliate programs like Clickbank or Amazon that are accessible to anyone. You get paid if someone clicks on a link to their products in your videos' description box.

How to Become a Successful Vlogger

Starting out may not be easy at first but with these guidelines, you have a rough road map to follow.

1.   First thing to consider is the topic for your blog; the best way is to find something you are passionate about. It is your passion that will drive the business; it is passion that will make it easy for you to come up with new video post ideas. You don't have to limit yourself to just one topic, although vlogs that focus on one particular topic (or a small group of related topics) tend to do better and they attract loyal and dedicated followers. It is better to choose a niche that you are familiar with already.

Vlogging is not all about educating people on a particular subject—being comfortable with what you are willing to share with the world is the important factor here. Many decide to share their daily life experiences while others create step by step guides for DIY activities.

The main thing I have noticed about the most successful vlogs is that the vloggers are real people who are sharing real life experiences. In doing so, they become educators who are witty, funny and sometimes even thought-provoking. Overall, they express their passions and their true personalities.

2.   Next, you need a camera with great video and audio playback; sometimes you may require a tripod for balancing. You'll also need a computer with video editing software and of course the right content. The right content will ultimately be the best selling point. Find something you can relate intelligently and in an interesting manner. This will guarantee repeat visits from a regular audience and will increase your viewers' loyalty. If you are promoting a product, the objective should be to create content that would create awareness for the product and encourage sales.

As your views go up, so will your subscribers. It is important to continuously post videos because that will solidify your vlog as something that is continuous. Many give up in the starting stage because of the low views. But what you have to understand is that every time you make a video, it has roots that are growing beneath your channel. Eventually those roots will experience a sudden jump that will cause you to get lots of views for your videos. But all of this will only happen with consistency and dedication. Ultimately, it is the number of views that would eventually create that 6 figure income.

3.   Promote your vlog post. You can utilize other social media channels to promote your posts. For added search engine optimization, use Google Instant to research keywords in your niche. Integrate key words into your topic and tags so that your videos show up at the top on search engines.

Google Instant is the embedded search bar feature on the

Google Search Engine that tries to help you complete your sentence when typing into the search bar. This gives an insight into what users are searching for within your niche. It is VERY important to use keywords in your research.

How to Setup your Vlog Channel

Once you have settled on what you want to share with the world, you can now follow these steps to create an account with YouTube and publish your videos.

Log on to YouTube and click "Create Account" on the top right-hand corner of the screen. This will lead you to the Google Accounts page, where you will fill in all the necessary fields to create a Google account that will also be your YouTube account. If you already have a Google account, you also have a Youtube account—you just need to sign in using your gmail ID and password.

1.   Sign on to YouTube

2.   Setup your account and upload your videos

3.   Enable monetization of your video

4.   Create your AdSense account

Keynotes

After you have followed the steps above, you can now publish your videos. You will be required to provide information about its content, as this will help Google push the right ads to your video, which will allow you to make some money. You should also fill in the descriptive information of your video. Remember to use catchy titles, common tags and relevant keywords. This will help with the SEO of your channel.

Finally, proceed to promote your video within your network on social media and encourage others to share your post. You can also post the video's link on forums you go to, as well as email the link to different bloggers and ask them to post it on their sites. The more your posts are shared on the Internet, the more traffic you are likely to drive to the video.

Do not relent in continuing to make videos and promoting them. You can schedule a regular marketing strategy or take advantage of services that will help in the promotion of your channel for a small fee.

Making a profitable vlog requires hard work, dedication and time. So I would implore you to go into this with the right mindset and expectations. Set realistic goals and pursue those goals with adequate and targeted action. When in doubt, or if you get stuck, you can always visit forums for solutions to challenges; chances are you're not the only vlogger out there who is experiencing them.

The opportunities are enormous. I have seen people make money just after a few days of launching their channel. The key is to understanding how to drive traffic. Take it slow, and one day at a time. Pursue knowledge and follow those who have gotten it right and I assure you, you will not lose track.

If you play your cards right, depending on your niche and how much traffic you can drive to your vlog, you could start making money with your video blog anywhere from 3 months to 1 year.

CHAPTER 14 - GHOST WRITING

Ghost writers are freelance writers who are hired to write books for a one-time fee. Generally, the services of a ghost writer are requested for rewriting website content, business copywriting, or other writing for personal or professional use. The ghost is usually hired with an agreement that he or she will not disclose who wrote the content to the public.

The hirer or author takes credit for all original work produced as the ghost writer has been paid an upfront fee already. The ghost writer takes no credit for the work produced as it is no longer considered to be his or her intellectual property.

This may sound odd, but it is a practice that is quite common and has been around for a while now. When authors, notable people, busy executives and authorities in certain fields want something written or are looking to publish a literary work, they turn to a professional freelance writer to help them deliver a sparkling, well written write-up.

Sometimes, on some rare occasion, the ghostwriter gets a mention as a co-author or editor in a book he or she has written. This is sometimes due to an agreement that is made between the hirer and the ghost writer, in which the ghost writer agrees to a lower upfront fee in exchange for a certain percentage of proceeds from the sale of the book.

How much do Ghost writers earn?

Depending on the literary work to be produced and the writers pedigree, the ghost writer can charge fees of anywhere from $10 to $25,000.

Ghostwriters are usually hired for the quality of work they deliver and there are different kinds of deals a ghost writer can make with the book author to ensure a fair deal for both parties when the contract is signed.

How to Become a Ghost Writer

In order to become a ghost writer of repute, you must first have experience as a freelance writer or experience writing almost anything. Preferably, you should have paid experience in website copywriting and other forms of copywriting for businesses. Most people have written essays in school or college. It may be a good idea to brush up on your writing skills before setting out on this career.

Before I delve into the practical aspects of how you can become a ghostwriter, let us consider why you should add "Ghostwriter" to your writing services:

1.   You'll get paid up front.

2.   It's lucrative. With the right clients, you can earn more than you would in other writing services you provide.

3.   There is absolutely no need for marketing. This means you can proceed to the next project ASAP.

4.   The ghostwriter is exposed to a wide scope of subject areas that he or she ordinarily would not have explored. Sometimes, the right client comes along, and the work will transport you through uncharted paths or information you didn't know before, and you will expand your general knowledge. It is a fascinating experience for those who talk about it.

5.   Ghostwriting will consistently challenge your writing skills. It will make you a better writer. Because you are constantly writing, it is only natural that you would just

continue to get better at it.

Becoming a great ghostwriter is a combination of patience, determination, experience, confidence, marketing and luck. Here's how to get started in this profession:

1.   Gain experience

One of the practical ways you can become a better freelance Ghost writer is to gather enough experience through writings for Journals, Blogs, and publications. Make insightful comments on websites or even self-publish a book. It is important you write and write some more. As you gain experience and exposure, you may catch the attention of busy CEOs and executives who need writers to write in their name.

2.   Hone your skills

It is said that the best writers are the best readers. In becoming a professional ghost writer, you have to develop the habit of reading. In the words of Stephen King, "If you don't have time to read, you don't have the time (or the tools) to write—simple as that." Read classics, today's popular books, newsletters and magazines. Practice and learn how to tell a compelling story. Read books that show you how to get better at your craft including titles such as "How to Read Better" or "How to Speed Read".

3.   Be patient

It will surely take a while and lots of practice to become a great freelance ghostwriter. Initially you may get small tasks that do not earn you much money. But as you progress, you will begin to see larger and more profitable tasks. Continue to write and expand your network by reaching out to possible clients. Publish your works on social platforms for criticism; it will only help you get better. Learning is constant. In the words of Ernest Hemingway, "We are all apprentices in a craft where no one ever becomes a master."

4.   Sell Your Skill

You can try setting up your own website and offering ghostwriting services that way or you can choose to use existing freelancer websites like upwork.com. Either way, you will need to get the word out there just like any other business.

5.   Get lucky

A lot of Ghost writers have said they had to work on smaller writing projects before "getting lucky" and breaking into ghostwriting:

Mike Loomis ran a multimedia book and product marketing business before realizing he could help authors through ghostwriting services.

Disadvantages of Ghostwriting:

1.   There are authors looking to take advantage of you. Because they know that most new ghost writers are itching to get to work, they convince you to accept a large body of work for a very minimal fee. This can sometimes be frustrating along the way as the burden of turning out good work starts to weigh on you. It is important you have representation during negotiation if you know you won't be able to handle the pressure.

2.   You are at the clients' mercy for referrals and reviews. If you do a good job, your client is expected to refer you to other clients or provide a review. That is how it is supposed to work. However, this is not in your control. You may deal with

a client who is not willing to share your contact to others or ends up giving you a poor review.

3.   You may not have the opportunity to build a brand. Since you are always hiding in the shadows, as the years roll by, you may start to lose the appeal, it is your brand that keeps your name alive. In the age of authorship, being anonymous won't help your career.

Smart ghostwriters have learned how to bank off the growing success of their clients by incorporating royalties into their contracts. So if your client's work becomes a bestseller or you're bringing traffic to their blog, you reap the benefits of that success.

CHAPTER 15 - VIRTUAL ASSISTANT

One of the easiest ways to work from home is to be a virtual assistant. It is called being a VA in short form and is a popular occupation for many across the world. A virtual assistant is a skilled, home-based professional who offers administrative support to companies, businesses and entrepreneurs through the Internet.

Virtual assistants perform a wide range of tasks depending on the training, experience and skillset they have acquired over time. Becoming a virtual assistant is a good option for those who wish to work from home. This work allows for a measure of freedom whilst providing you with a stable income. There is also the advantage of "no loss". You cannot really lose money as you are not investing money into a traditional-type business.

The scope of a virtual assistant goes beyond sitting behind a desk and completing a task on the computer. You could act as a mail reader, schedule organizer, errand runner, representative of business or client and the list goes on. You do not need a lot of specialist knowledge as most of the tasks will only require general knowledge. However, you should ensure that you can complete a task before accepting to do it. It helps maintain integrity and eliminates the risk of disgruntled clients. If you think you will need training, do not hesitate to ask your clients. Most clients will provide you with a document or a video training material for the tasks they want you to complete.

Getting Started

Employee or entrepreneur

Whatever choice you make, there are rules to follow to become successful. When you work as an employee, you don't have to invest any money or find your own clients. You just register with an agency and they will send tasks to you to complete. Like every other job, your work hours and how much you perform is limited to what your agency offers you in a given time.

On the other hand, if you decide to set up your own business, everything will be on your terms. This means the choice of clients, your schedule and your rates will all be under your own control. You would also need to promote yourself and find clients.

The things needed to set up a virtual assistant business include a phone, computer and the Internet. If you fancy networking, are an entrepreneur at heart, like being in charge and having full control, I recommend that you become an independent virtual assistant. On the other hand, if you like being able to pinch in and out, having someone else find clients and just tell you where and when to show up, then applying to an agency would be better. Agencies can be found through a google search in your country and they usually are regularly seeking virtual assistants to join their ranks and serve customers.

Finding a Market

If you have chosen the entrepreneurial route, then you need to find clients. One way to do so is to setup a website advertising your skill sets and what you can do. This is very important, asides from looking out for a client; you can make it a hotbed for information. Research and write on topic that is interesting and would attract visitors. The benefits are two folds.

1.   Your website becomes a place to show your skills and competence. Clients get a first-hand feel of what your service is like before committing to giving you a job. You will need reviews and testimonials on your website so you can convince others easily.

2.   You can take advantage of other ways to earn money online. You can use your website to promote affiliate products and register it for Google AdSense or any of the numerous pay per click Ad networks.

Freelance Platforms

There are a lot of online platforms that link virtual assistants with clients. The two popular platforms are Upwork.com and Fiverr.com. On a freelance platform, you are expected to create a profile and sell your skills to prospective clients. The market is very competitive here as there are a lot of people offering similar services at different prices that may not be to your liking. In order to get your own rate for the work you do and still have lots of clients, you must be willing to stand out.

One of the ways you can stand out is to offer value added services or unique services that are rarely being offered. This attracts clients to you as they are promised more value for their money. Other clients that have a specific requirement will post a job on these platforms. You can check daily what people are posting to get an idea of what kind of services are in demand. You can then post your own jobs based on the data you collect on a daily or weekly basis.

Training

A virtual assistant is expected to be organized. You should possess good time management skills. You should also have great communication skills and be able to get work done properly as fast as possible.

Tips to Becoming a Successful Virtual Assistant

Time is of great importance to clients. Always stick to the deadlines. Develop excellent people skills and do not be afraid to get out of your comfort zone to help others. Always look out for ways to sell your services. Your ability to communicate in fluent English or any other language is an added advantage. Instant availability on platforms such as Skype will also set you apart from the crowd.

Invest in learning, look out for free and paid sources that will grow your skillset. Do not be afraid to ask questions from clients, especially if you think something may go wrong in the job you have taken. It is important to reply to any messages promptly as clients expect a response immediately. If you are busy, you can respond by saying "I have seen your message and will reply shortly. Your patience is appreciated."

Expected Income

As a virtual assistant, there are no exact figures stating how much you can earn but it is important to know that your earnings depend on the task, your client's view of the task and your portfolio. Virtual assistants with a lot of positive reviews tend to command higher fees. Assistants with some sort of specialist knowledge or skill also earn higher amounts. The average amount you wish to charge is ultimately up to you. Most virtual assistants charge $10 to $15 per hour of work.

As you set out, you should concentrate on building a profile first, invest in yourself and seek ways to set yourself apart from everyone else.

CHAPTER 16 - GOOGLE ADSENSE

Google AdSense is an ad network owned and operated by Google. As of today, it is the largest and highest paying ad network on the internet. Google AdSense is the program designed for website publishers who want to display targeted advertisements on their web pages and earn money when visitors view or click the ads.

Getting Started

To earn from Google AdSense, you will need to have a website or blog, although not all websites do well with AdSense. There are basically 2 key factors to consider if you want to make money with AdSense: you need great content and a lot of traffic.

There are also two types of website content: the one that attracts new visitors and the other that brings visitors returning daily. The ideal website for AdSense is one that is balanced for both. This ensures that just as you are attracting new visitors (traffic), you are also retaining loyal ones.

Examples of websites perfect for AdSense include but are not limited to: news blogs or websites, forums, niche sites, listicle blogs, how-to websites and online discussion boards. All you need is to find a layout that works well with displaying contents and AdSense ads.

It is important that you also understand the kinds of ads that AdSense will place on your website. Because advertisers have the options of creating ads in various formats (text-based, images, and/or video), you will need to create layouts that will accommodate the various formats, but ensure that they do not interfere with the content. The user always comes first.

Aside from display ads, AdSense offers another feature: custom search ads. This type of ad allows visitors to search for specific content on your website using AdSense. This is great because ads are displayed alongside the results of related searches.

Benefits of Google AdSense

There are various benefits of using Google AdSense aside from the fact that there are very few restrictions. It is easy to use, you get to earn consistent revenue from your websites and AdSense pays you on time.

How to make money for AdSense

To make money from AdSense, we have to first understand how AdSense calculates the earnings. We have to understand what CTR and CPC mean, what formula AdSense uses and how we can optimize the website or blog to get maximum benefits from AdSense.

CTR = Click Through Rate

This is the ratio of the number of users who click on an ad on a web page to the total number of visitors who visited the web page within a particular time frame. This is usually used to determine the effectiveness of advertisement on a website.

CPC = Cost Per Click

This is the amount earned by a website owner anytime a user clicks an advertisement on the web page. The earnings vary and it depends on the advertiser and niche, as some advertisers are willing to pay more than others.

The AdSense formula has 3 variables; Traffic, CTR and CPC.

The formula is recreated below.

Traffic x CTR x CPC = Revenue.

To ensure you continue to earn from AdSense, you have to find ways to increase any or all three of the variables. You can increase your CTR by placing your ads above the content. The higher your ads are, the greater the likelihood of increasing your CTR. You should also consider other factors like text color and size. You can increase your CPC by targeting high paying niches (Medical, Legal, etc.).

1.   Ad Placements

Where you place ads on your website determines how much you can benefit from Google AdSense. There are several locations on a web page where you can place ads for maximum visibility.

The header: this is above the content on the web page. It allows for maximum visibility and is most likely the ad with the highest CTR.

Between Paragraphs: This is also a great location for ads. Ensure you use a size of 300×250 for mobile and 728x90 for desktop.

Sidebar: Ads placed here also do pretty well. Use a 300x600 unit for both top and bottom sidebars.

Bottom of the content: Many website owners have reported great results from ads placed at the bottom of the content, especially when it was relevant to the content of their post.

2.   Increase Traffic

Traffic is the major determinant of how much you can make

with AdSense. The more traffic you get, the greater the likelihood of a better CTR. Other tweaks to increasing revenue are available but the most stable way is through traffic. There are several ways you can increase traffic and they include:

Create great content. Give people something worth their time. You don't have to be a master at writing quality articles or creating a great post, just be good at what you are offering. Your content doesn't have to be long, but let it be real. There are great travel blogs raking in big money from AdSense; they just share their travel experience but also make it very interesting and educational. This converts to great traffic when users share and invite others to visit. Those people eventually become regular readers and invite others, which creates a chain reaction.

3.   Keywords

Using the right keywords in your content would help drive organic traffic to your website. It would be a shame if after investing in great content, proper ad placement and all the necessary tweaks; you fail at attracting organic traffic due to a lack of appropriate keywords. Research keywords that are suitable for your content, find their ranks, and also check Google Trends to get an idea of popular keywords.

4.   Map out an Efficient Strategy

It is ideal that you have an original strategy that works for you. This helps you to keep focus on what you're interested in and what direction you want your business to go. There a couple of strategies you can adopt.

You can choose to create lots of content with string keywords that help you generate organic search traffic, or you can choose to focus on filling little pieces of content with "monster keywords". Whatever you are comfortable with and what works for you would be fine. In my opinion, creating great content with string keywords is usually the best approach. Aside from the value it creates for your users or visitors, you are likely to have repeat visits more often than from content with "monster keywords".

5.   AdSense is Not the Only Ad network

Ad networks such as Media.net and Alpha are gradually carving their own place in the ad network ecosystem. Diversifying your ad network also helps in case there are problems with AdSense or if you are banned. That way, you won't lose all of your money. Sometimes, you will find that these other ad networks are actually outperforming AdSense.

6.   Explore Other Offers

Do not get stuck working your website or blog to serve only AdSense. This practice of incorporating other online products and businesses is a good way to diversify and take great advantage of your platform. Do not aggressively pursue affiliate marketing to avoid the AdSense hammer but try still to diversify. Create content that promotes affiliate links but don't overdo it.

Mistakes to Avoid

There are a few mistakes to avoid when designing your layout to allow for AdSense. Avoid placing ads adjacent to images, next page buttons and in any way that would attract accidental clicks on your web page. This will cause you to avoid a penalty called the Nessie penalty.

The Nessie penalty is imposed by AdSense when you have an unusually high CTR. These accidental clicks can sometimes arise as a result of your layout or in some cases from your aggressive marketing. In all, it is advised that you try to keep your CTR as moderate as possible.

Conclusion

AdSense is a viable way to make serious money online with a website. The key is to building traffic and implementing the measures we have highlighted here. You are also required to regularly update your knowledge and implement a lot of new strategies to find out what works best for you. There is a lot of trial and error in any business, so do not become apprehensive if something fails at first. Keep trying and improving your strategy and it will eventually work out.

CHAPTER 17 - AFFILIATE MARKETING

If you love sales, then you should love affiliate marketing. Affiliate marketing gives you a chance to make money by promoting other people's products or services. When you refer a person to a website through your affiliate link, you get paid a commission if they purchase something or perform a specific action.

Affiliate marketing is one of the quickest and cheapest ways to make money online. However, that does not mean it has no disadvantages. There are pros and cons, just like with everything else.

Possible Challenges

There are a few challenges that can limit your chances of earning money from Google AdSense. For starters, getting approved has become a herculean task recently. The criteria are harder to meet and are not flexible. Your website has to meet certain standards of quality and traffic before you can get approved.

They have very strict terms of service, revenues are constantly fluctuating and there are lower revenues generated on mobile due to its limited space. Furthermore, there is the challenge of ad blockers and the worst of all, you can get banned! If your account is banned for whatever reason, you will lose all the money that was accrued in your account. All of your efforts could possibly be wasted.

How Does it Work?

Affiliate marketing is a marketing technique adopted by businesses to encourage sales and expand their market. For you, the affiliate marketer, you earn a commission based on the numbers of referrals you convert for the business. It may sound a little difficult but it is one of the most popular online businesses; the millions engaged in affiliate marketing will confirm its profitability. Finance blogger Michelle Schroeder (www.makingsenseofcents.com) was interviewed in 2016 and she said that she makes about $50,000 monthly from affiliate marketing alone on her blog. She is one of the many successful examples out there.

To get involved in affiliate marketing, you have to sign up for an affiliate program, and choose the products you want to promote. The merchant will then provide you with a unique affiliate code; that is the code/link that you will use to refer customers to the merchant's website in order to earn a commission and get paid. You can track your performance, stats and commissions in real time using your unique affiliate ID on the platform of your affiliate program.

There are various programs for affiliate marketing. Not all involve the sale of products. Some may only require that a person provides information about themselves (i.e. fills out a short contact form) while others may insist on a sale before you can earn any commissions. The various programs are listed below for better understanding.

Pay per Sale: In this program, you earn a percentage on the sale whenever a purchase is made.

Pay per Click: this program is strictly for re-directs. Your earnings are based on the number of visitors you redirect from your website to the merchant's website. They don't have to purchase anything before you earn.

Pay per Lead: This is strictly used for lead generation. You only earn when the referred visitor provides his or her contact information on the target site by filling out a contact form.

Website or No Website

When people think of affiliate marketing, many imagine managing a website or blog, building an email list, and trying to drive traffic to it. It would definitely help if you have a blog or website because it will give you that grounded feeling. You will have a place where all of your efforts will be brought together. You can use an email list to promote your products easily. But there are also other ways.

You can become an affiliate marketer without having a website or a blog. Social media is a great way to start and it allows you to test your strategies before making an investment to setup a website. You can make use of Facebook, Instagram and YouTube. The key here is not to spam. For instance, if you are a fitness enthusiast, create a page dedicated to fitness on Facebook, show your workouts in pictures and videos, and then utilize the opportunity to promote (affiliate) workout gears.

This works great for most programs and won't get you thrown out from the social media platform. Aside from these reasons, it is also a great way to build a subscriber base and drive traffic to your page as people are encouraged to return to your page. The same applies to Instagram and YouTube.

There are several affiliate programs that are newbie friendly, although you may be required to go through an acceptance screening, because affiliate marketing is a serious business. Affiliate marketplaces like Commission Junction, Shareasale, and Rakuten bring together advertisers with affiliate programs and publishers like you who are looking for products to promote. Amazon is also one of the major affiliate marketplaces but we shall be discussing that later in a subsequent section.

How to Become a Successful Affiliate Marketer

First off, Affiliate marketing is not a stroll in the park. It can eventually become passive but it is still a serious business when you are starting out. If you want maximum results from this opportunity, then you have to put in the work.

The attraction to affiliate marketing stems from features such as little or no overhead, no logistics and can be started from home. This and many other reasons have drawn millions to affiliate marketing but there are a few things that differentiate a successful affiliate marketer from the one who is struggling to gain traction. In order to succeed, you have to understand how affiliate marketing works and the importance of creating value through content. You must use proper marketing strategies and channels for you to become successful.

In essence, there are two parts to affiliate marketing. The first is acquisition of leads and the second is promotion to those leads. If any of the two parts fails, the entire business does not work. The following are steps you need to take to create your own affiliate marketing business. We will not discuss creating a website here. There are solution providers like WordPress and Tumblr that offer a one-click service for that.

Choose the correct niche: According to research, the most popular niches include health and fitness, fashion and finance. That is not to say that there are no affiliate products in other niches. Research keywords, find out what's trending, find a good spot where you can thrive and you will be successful.

Create Value Through Content: Most affiliate programs require you to have content when placing links. Search engine bots have become smarter as they only help websites with real content. It will help your brand a great deal if you offer valuable content in the course of conducting your business.

Let's assume you have enrolled in a program to promote a brand of facial scrub. You can create content and add value by creating a short video on Facebook and teaching those in your network how to use the product. You can also offer free tips on maintaining great facial skin on a regular basis. Make your page, website, or blog a hub for information on facial care that updates regularly.

Here's another example. Let's say you are promoting car insurance, you can add value by offering tips and guides on picking the right insurance for cars. You can also educate on specific areas like maintenance and provide information to race car enthusiasts.

Marketing Strategies and Channels

It is a very good idea to use different product promotion strategizes so you can figure out what is working and what is not. Measure the performance of each campaign and take proper action. Changing a few things here and there can increase your profit dramatically. Most affiliate marketers tend to put up their ads and links only on their websites. There is nothing wrong with this approach, but there are other sources of generating traffic to your affiliate products. Like we have discussed earlier, you should be using social networking sites like Facebook, Twitter, Pinterest, Google+ and Instagram. The more targeted traffic you can push to your sales page the better your chances of making money.

Google AdWords is good tool to drive targeted traffic to a sales page. Just be mindful of the cost to run the campaign versus the revenue from the same campaign to ensure that the venture is a profitable one. AdWords has tools to monitor these things; you will do well to use them.

Most affiliate programs will provide you with the basic stats that you will need to run your program effectively. You can also invest in a conversion tracking software. There a lot of those on the internet free to use but I would suggest you purchase a premium. Try to keep abreast with new techniques and market trends.

Choose the Right Merchant

Choose wisely! You don't want to have unhappy customers or hurt your brand. Stick with websites and companies that offer good customer service.

Once you're set up, don't sit idly waiting for customers. Promote yourself utilizing all channels, paid or free. Get as much exposure as you can muster. Have a plan and stick with it; offer value to returning customers and collect information by conducting surveys. This will help you to know what you should be doing and what you should avoid. It would also help you to build your email list because it is the best and most effective tool for marketing.

Lastly, tools like Affiliate Link Manager (a plugin that can be integrated with your WordPress site) can assist with managing your affiliate accounts.

CHAPTER 18 - SHOPIFY

While we have discussed an ecommerce store before, it is beneficial to have a chapter on Shopify just because of the advantages it presents. It is a Canadian company that has allowed many to build their online physical product business to a level where they are generating huge revenues. Some successful examples of brands and stores on this platform include:

1) A Book Apart: this is an online publishing company that does more than $100,000 every year in sales.
2) Taylor Stitch: This company sells custom clothing for men which is tailored to their specific needs. In 2013, the revenue was over $1,000,000.
3) Goldieblox: This company sells educational toys and games online. In 2013, they did more than $290,000 per month.
4) Pure Cycle: this company made more than $3,000,000 in 2012 by selling bicycles.

Advantages of Using Shopify as compared to other online store options

When you are about to start an online store, you have many different options to consider. Shopify can be considered as the best option out of them. That's because Shopify offers some unique features, which you cannot get from the other platforms that can be used to set up an online store. Here is a list of some of the most prominent benefits delivered by Shopify.

- Shopify is extremely easy to set up and use. You can do it on your own, even if you don't have a good technical background.

- Shopify is a reliable and a secure platform available for you to create an online store.

- Shopify provides 24/7 customer support to you and you can quickly resolve the issues that you come across.

- Shopify can be considered as a mobile friendly platform and you don't need to go through any extra efforts to make it mobile responsive.

- Shopify can be customized as per your specific needs and requirements.

- Shopify is compatible with some of the best marketing and SEO tools. Therefore, you can easily enhance the visibility of your online store.

How to Setup Your Shopify Store

As mentioned earlier, any person can use Shopify with ease and enjoy all the benefits offered by it. Here is a step by step guide, which you will have to follow in order to setup your Shopify store.

- First of all, you will need to sign up for a Shopify account. After the sign up, you will be able to create the basic structure of your store as well.

- Secondly, you will have to add a product to the Shopify store that you created.

- Now you have a basic functioning Shopify store and you will have to customize the look and make it beautiful.

- You will need to configure a domain for the Shopify store.

- As the last step, you will need to configure a payment processor, so that you can accept customer payments.

Driving Traffic to Your Shopify Store

Congratulations! Now you are the owner of an online store powered by Shopify. As the next step, you should drive traffic towards your store. There are few effective strategies available for you to follow in order to drive traffic to the Shopify store as well.

Search Engine Optimization can be considered as the best method available for you to drive traffic towards Shopify store. Since Shopify is SEO friendly, you will not have to go through a lot of hassle in order to bring it up on the search engine results. You just need to learn the basics of SEO and you will be able to attract potential buyers to your store.

You can also try social media marketing because it is another proven method available to drive traffic towards the Shopify store. This is one of the most cost effective methods available for you to make your store a popular one. You just need to run extensive campaigns on some of the most popular social media networks such as Facebook and Instagram. You will be amazed by the results that it can deliver to you within a short period of time. You can also ask your friends and family members to share the store. Word of mouth can also deliver effective contributions to the overall popularity of your Shopify store.

Handling Customer Service for Your Orders

Now you are getting a decent amount of customers for your online store. You need to transform them into long lasting customers, so that your online store can benefit from constant revenue from them in the future. In order to do that, you should offer a top notch service for all of the customers.

You can offer customer service through multiple channels. Some of the best channels available for you to offer customer service include phone, helpdesk, live chat, social media and emails. It is always recommended for you to respond to customer concerns within the shortest possible time. If you cannot do it, you should simply outsource your customer support. Then you will be able to impress your customers and they will continue to shop at your store for years to come.

CHAPTER 19 - LISTICLE BLOGGING

A listicle is a blog post or article found on the web which is outlined in a bullet point or numbered fashion. Listicles have become the current rave and now we have entire websites and blogs made just out of them. Although listicles have been around for a long time, they have only regained popularity in recent times. Their purpose is to engage readers and provide information in a fast manner. The term "listicle blogging" is dedicated to entire blogs that are made solely in a list format.

Studies have shown that when people search for information, they prefer to read information that is presented in a step by step format, such as a list. It is believed that this format allows for easy perusal and digestion of the information. In fact, the title of this book is written in a listicle format.

Instruction specialist Abreena Tompkins conducted a research analysis about online learning and concluded that information grouped in parcels of three or five can better help people absorb information faster.

How is Money Made?

Like normal blogging, you can make passive income from advertising, affiliate marketing, and most of all, from selling a product or service.

The major selling point of a listicle blog is the catchy nature of it. For instance; you must have seen articles that are titled similar to the following:

15 Top Reasons to Visit Brazil.

7 Mistakes Most Bloggers Make.

5 Reasons to Use Listicle Blogging.

What emotions do these titles cause the reader to feel? Curiosity. You want to find out what the writer has in store. It also tells you what to expect; if there are seven mistakes bloggers are making, then you know when the list of mistakes are going to end; you can estimate how much time it will take you to get through the article, and how much information you will have to process. Listicle blogging is one of the fastest growing blogging niches.

Creating Your Listicle

In quick steps, we shall be examining 7 rules to follow when setting up a listicle blog.

1.   Pick your topics carefully. Ensure you have adequate information and resources on whatever topic you choose to write on. It is advisable that you think broadly about the information you want to put out as you need to make your post clear and concise. Be sure to pick unique and interesting topics or elements, topics that your readers may not know about or are interested in knowing more about. Mention new ideas in your posts so your readers do not get bored.

2.   When you have picked your topic and have adequate information, you should begin as planned but still be responsive to change. For example, if you initially set out to write about 10 great ideas but later found more resources such that you can now write 30 ideas, then it is better to change the plan and write about the 30 ideas instead. Studies conducted by the industry-leader Moz on different types of content that generated backlinks and social shares revealed that long form content (articles longer than 1000 words) received more shares and links than shorter-form content. This was

especially true when the larger content was more detailed and easy to follow.

3.   Choose the format for your blog. There are three main formats, namely:

Ranking: This process determines the position of items on the list. The list should be based on merit, or it can take the shape of a hierarchy (e.g. from worst to best), or deadliest, or most interesting, or least creepy, etc.

List Theme: You can write about a particular subject of appeal, but make sure that it has a theme. Let the theme reflect the essence of the article.

Random list: Lacking in both theme or ranking, this is where you just throw ideas around and leave the readers to draw their own conclusions. This is best left to a good writer as it can sometimes lead the reader to become irritated by the lack of conclusions.

4.   Write with the conscious intent to engage. Content is still the main selling point. Let your writing style be catchy, witty and informative. Use pictures to better tell your story. Post articles that get people excited and motivated. You can also share an inspirational post on your listicle blog to motivate your readers.

5.   Get controversial. You can choose a controversial topic and lure your audience in until they are emotionally engaged and begin to discuss the topic on your blog. But please be careful, do it in moderation as it may get you some backlash. Make sure *you are properly and fully educated on the topic you choose to take on.*

6.   Finally, keep your post titles short and sweet. This is

one of the reasons Twitter has grown in popularity. An average internet user has an attention span of about 7.5 seconds. Most importantly, try to stay away from complex sounding titles that hamper your message and confuse your audience.

If you follow these steps, you are almost guaranteed success. Information on how to set up a blog has been extensively covered in the previous sections. The other points mentioned in the chapter for blogging can also be applied here to generate income.

CHAPTER 20 - ONLINE COURSES

Taking an online video course is a great way to make money from the internet. Anyone with some sort of skill or hobby can teach. You just require sufficient knowledge to pass onto someone else who wants to learn. Whether your skills include playing an instrument, graphics design, computer programming or do-it-yourself expertise, then creating an online course and selling it to others can be something to explore.

Lots of people on the internet are looking for those who have **real experience** in completing a certain task and who can actually teach others. This is why they are willing to pay for the service. Take note of the emphasis on "real experience". Most of what you would be teaching is available for free on the internet, but the real idea here is that a lot of people would rather pay for someone who has real experience, and can show them in steps how to perform those tasks. Now what would set you apart is the kind of experience you have and the amount of knowledge you possess on the particular skill.

You don't require any teaching experience to sell online courses; if you do have some experience, it is fine and an added advantage but it is not a prerequisite.

Online marketplace exists where you can create your courses and publish for students who need it. Platforms like Udemy and Skillshare are the most popular, with Udemy attracting over 9 million students from over 190 countries. This should give you an idea about the kind of reach you can have. Platforms like Teachable allow you to create your own online classroom.

How much money can I make?

Once you create and publish your courses; it is advisable you create more than one course and have a large portfolio. The opportunity for earning from them is limitless. Then, you can just create a buzz around your courses and earn. Some courses may require you to refresh your knowledge if you have not looked at them recently. Other than that, the only actions you need to be concerned about are marketing and driving traffic. Most courses sell for $10 - $500 depending on the volume, the type of knowledge being sold and the popularity of the instructor.

An important point to mention here is that your students will have lots of questions. It is advisable that you create a specific group (such as on Facebook) just for your students. This way, they can ask questions and other members can help them if they know the answer. As you gain traction, you can increase the price of your courses and earn even more.

Getting Started

The main task is to decide what to teach and how to make your videos. It is advisable to do research and see other successful online courses in the area you are about to take on. It will help you because you can learn from the mistakes of existing instructors.

Format of teaching

There are different options available that you can include in your teaching. Use scenarios, illustrations and examples to aid understanding. If your course work involves practical steps, you could create videos in which you practically analyze the steps.

For instance, let's say I decide to teach design (stencil cutting) on Udemy. My coursework will involve both screencasts (showing the process of designing my stencils) and the actual cutting of the stencils. I will be as clear as I can be, showing the students the different methods to cut stencils and maybe a more efficient method I discovered from my years of experience. That is basically the idea of structuring a course. It should flow well and aid understanding.

Making your Videos

After deciding on what to teach, you have to create a structure. It is your course structure or outline that will determine the kind of video style you will use. There are 3 types of styles including the Screencast, Talking head and a combination of both.

Screencast: In this method, you teach while showing only your computer screen with your voice in the background. This style is relatively inexpensive to use as you can shoot from home and do everything by yourself. Editing the videos is also quite easy. There are various software like Camtasia that will help you create a professional looking video.

Talking head: You may require the services of a studio to achieve this. Lighting is of great importance here because it involves taking shots of you teaching the course. This style is advisable if you have to show practical examples. Courses that require this style by default are courses related to learning a practical skill like playing an instrument. If you are strapped for cash and do not have enough to pay for a studio, you can use a clear space in your home. You will have to ensure that the environment is well lighted, otherwise you can finish off any inconsistencies with video editing. It is advisable that you develop great video editing skills as they will save you a lot of money in the long run.

A mix of both: This is the best style to use in my opinion. It helps to cover all facets of the course outline and also helps to create a connection between the instructor and the user. The idea is that during the course of the video, you get to show the screen and also the image of the instructor. It works for all course types, although it will require an advanced knowledge of video production and editing.

You can start with the screencast and then as you get a hang of it and improve your editing and video production skills, you can explore by mixing both styles.

Promoting your course

Online marketplaces like Udemy and Skillshare help you to promote courses on their platform. You still have to do marketing on your own, since you cannot rely solely on their algorithms. If there is a change made in the algorithm, you may not show up for a specific search result. This is why it is a good idea to diversify your marketing and sources of traffic.

To successfully market and promote your course, you will need to look towards other social media platforms. One platform that has proven to be very effective is YouTube. Having free videos on YouTube that add value can help convert viewers to customers. Your YouTube channel should be a great platform to advertise your course. You should create teaser videos of no more than 3 minutes long, highlighting the key part of your course outline and inviting the viewer to enroll on any of the online course marketplaces that host your course. The same strategy should be applied to Facebook and Instagram even though Instagram allows only about 1 minute of video. Being active and answering questions of forums like quora.com can also help build a following. Just spread your reach, look out for others who are doing similar things and learn from them.

Conclusion - Go Conquer!

Online courses are very lucrative. The major hurdle is creating the course; once you have covered that, you can register and upload your course on any of the online course marketplaces and earn. The cost is usually a one-time investment but I would advise that you create content that would have the user coming back for updates. This way you will have a steady flow of income.

There are a lot of possibilities with online courses. Connecting with a worldwide audience through education is one of the many advantages. I've personally had students from different parts of world; this can never happen in the traditional classroom.

If you feel like taking on a challenge, you can create your own website and host your courses on them. Platforms like Teachable will provide you with all the resources you need to execute that, leaving your viewers with a professional-looking platform. Here you have greater control. You can better monetize your videos this way too.

Teaching is now a well-paid profession. Some teachers now earn as much as $100,000 yearly from teaching courses online. With a large following, you can explore the possibility of subtle adverts and affiliate marketing, but don't overdo it.

Remember, the best teachers are those who know their story and also know how to tell it. They are not experts or gurus; just some cool dudes trying to make a difference. They are normal people who want to share their knowledge. I reckon

113

that they are just like you.

CHAPTER 21 - INTERNET MARKETING

Internet marketing is one of the most expansive niches in the online business ecosystem. You would have noticed by now how all of the businesses are linked some way, with certain differences. Internet marketing is one business that covers them all, as there is no business – online or offline, that doesn't require marketing on the internet.

According to TN Media, online (internet) marketing is "...any online tool, strategy or method of getting the company name out to the public. The advertisements can take many different forms and some strategies focus on subtle messages rather than clear-cut advertisements."

To explain internet marketing in simpler terms, we can say that it is the maximum number of marketing activities that can be done online. This includes activities such as affiliate marketing, email marketing, social media marketing, blogging, paid marketing, search engine optimization, etc. Basically, it is anything that you do on the Internet to get more visibility or to get others to buy from you.

The key to your making money on the internet is to first understand how the digital ecosystem works, and how internet businesses and ecommerce work in general. You have to dive in armed with correct information. The purpose of this guide is to provide you with the right information before you to take the plunge.

Getting Started

Internet marketing is a number of things and you can only achieve true success in your endeavor if you possess a wide range of skills required to succeed at the highest level. There is a need to look into the activities of those who have gone before us and have made it big on the internet. We have to find out from them what to do, what not to do and how to do it.

Let us examine one widely known and very successful internet marketer by the name of David Sharpe who was profiled by forbes.com.

Before Sharpe ever delved into the world of Internet marketing, he had a job as a construction worker. Like millions of other people around the world, he sought to make ends meet in the regular 9 to 5 jobs with a guaranteed paycheck at the end of the week. But try as he might, he was never able to actually get ahead, until he discovered Internet marketing.

In the beginning, like all new endeavors, it was rough. It took years to go from an absolute beginner to a seasoned sought-after professional. He has regularly stated that if he could do it, anyone could do it. However, in order to become the next David Sharpe, there are quite a few steps that you need to take.

There's a whole lot of information to grasp, and this guide may not cover all but it will provide you with the prerequisite knowledge to get you started. It is also important that you set your expectations right and stay persistent. It is important to remind yourself not to give up and get overwhelmed with all that is involved.

What Internet Marketing Is About and How Money Is Made

Internet marketing is an all-encompassing set of marketing activities done online. Your task is usually to promote affiliate products, services and programs across various channels and also to build the marketing campaigns for select brands across your network.

Most people don't actually know how good money is made on the Internet, how Facebook generates revenue or even Google. How do blogs become so popular and how do they generate money from all of that traffic? Is there one way or many?

The answer is quite simple, create value! The more value you create, the more successful you become. At the beginning, you have to focus more on creating value than on building revenue streams. That is how Facebook and Google both became tremendously successful. They didn't focus on revenues at the outset but on creating and delivering a high-value service. They knew they had to first offer something worthwhile before putting a price on it.

How to Become a Successful Internet Marketer

1.   Choose Your Business

Once you understand how everything works and you have the right expectations, you can now decide on what business you want to delve into. Do you want to become an affiliate marketer? Do you want to be a network marketer? Do you want to become a blogger and sell your own products? Or make Squeeze pages, sales pages that attract people and direct their attention towards providing their email address? Squeeze pages are created in a variety of ways. The better they are, the more likely they'll convert.

The key here is to understand that whatever you plan on doing, you are going to need a lot of traffic. You will need to devise ways to drive traffic to your offers if you want them to convert. One of the many ways you can do this is to leverage your social media contacts, share your links on blogs and websites, visit forums that are within your niche and make posts that all have your links redirecting to a landing page or squeeze page. This is where new people will come into contact with your business first and may eventually become customers.

If your chosen business is affiliate marketing, you will need to have a lot of targeted traffic if you are to make any real money. The affiliate offers also need to provide a high commission to you on each sale. You mut also ensure that the returns or chargebacks for those products or services are low. The last thing you want is to sell a product or service that provides very little value and gets returned often.

If you go with network marketing, understand that you need to get close to the top of the food chain, or your ability to generate any serious amount of income will be limited. You need to put in a lot of work and be wary of the hype and the sales pitches that get you thinking that it's going to work the other way. I would avoid Multi Level Marketing (MLM) companies as many are known to be pyramid schemes.

Email marketing? Sure. You can do that. But you'll need to build a massive and targeted list. You can start out by buying email lists from platforms like Fiverr, where freelancers offer to perform data mining services. Some of them will offer to check Linkedin and get you targeted emails. It is a good way to start when you don't have many emails.

2. Setup your own website

Your own website will become an online hub. It could be a blog or website but whatever you decide on, it has to be catchy. This is where your anchor content will "go live" on, everything else will link to that point. All the ads you run and traffic you drive through social media or SEO or anything else will all come here. You need a custom domain and a professional looking site if you want anyone to take you seriously.

You can buy a domain name from Godaddy even though there are cheapter alternatives. I prefer Godaddy because the dashboard is simple and you get regular email notices about your subscriptions or things you have signed up for. You also get reminders when your domain name is about to expire or if it will automatically get renewed.

After you have your own domain name, you can either outsource the building of the website to a freelancer or use a platform yourself. The most popular platform is wordpress as there are many plugins that make your life easier. There is also Weebly, which has great click-and-drop features that you can use to build your own website. It is important to keep updating your website so that your customers stay engaged.

3.   Promotion Channels

Like in all endeavors of life, good communication is very important. The information and how it is relayed are both vital in the equation. From the outset, it is important that you decide on how you will reach or communicate with your potential customers. Will you be blogging? Will you use social media as your primary method? Will you build a list by working with solo ad providers? Or will you place paid advertisements? Whatever you decide and how you hope to go about it, one thing is clear: you must become a guru copywriter. The better you are at copywriting, the more success you'll find as an Internet marketer.

By now, you are likely to have seen all the "experts" on your

Facebook and Instagram feed. Some are more popular than others. But the key thing to notice in the ads is that the ones with the most views and engagements are the most successful. Use a website like Similar Web to study those ads and see what they're doing. Join their lists and embed yourself in their funnels. This is an important part of the process. The plan here is to understand what the most successful marketers are doing and try to replicate them.

David Sharpe, who presently runs an online company called Legendary Marketer, teaches you how to duplicate his results. By understanding how Sharpe has constructed his value chain, positioned his offerings and built his multi-modality sales funnels, you you will be able to replicate the process in your own business.

Conclusion

There is a need for you to constantly educate yourself while you are on your way to becoming an Internet marketer of great reputation. The business is constantly evolving, the ways and techniques are constantly changing, so you need to continue to keep abreast with the latest trends, develop relationships with top marketers in your field, look into what they are doing and learn from it. The opportunities are enormous, it is your mindset and effor that will set you apart.

CHAPTER 22 - AMAZON AFFILIATE (ASSOCIATE)

We have covered affiliate marketing extensively in a previous section but because the Amazon Associates program is such a wonderful and very lucrative affiliate marketing program, there is a full section explaining how you can take advantage of it.

There are a lot of ways you can make money with Amazon, like selling items on the Amazon store or ebooks on Kindle and CreateSpace. However, one of the most interesting ways you can get started on Amazon is as an Amazon affiliate. These are a few reasons why being an Amazon affiliate is one of the best ways to make money on Amazon:

1) It is free to join

2) There are low startup costs

3) The business model is quite simple

It's completely free to join the Amazon Associates program. As long as you have a website, you can apply! If you don't have a website, not to worry, we will be covering the right type of website you need to help you generate the most money.

If you do not have a website, you can set one up on WordPress. It costs very little to have your website up and running in 5 minutes. Your total cost per month from a popular host such as Bluehost comes to about $20 a month and you require only very little knowledge of website design to tweak your website to suit your preference.

Being an Amazon affiliate is budget friendly as you don't stock or hold inventory, you are not required to buy goods, and you don't have to deal with any logistics such as shipping and delivery. The best part is that the process is fully automated.

Getting Started

There are a couple of steps you need to take to get started and be successful as an Amazon affiliate.

Build a Website: There are lots of online platforms that offer a one-click service. WordPress and Tumblr offer a ready-built framework for affiliate marketers. However, you will be required to acquire some knowledge on website design to help tweak your website for better functionality and great user experience.

Research Content: After designing your website, you need to create content that will bring in the users. Amazon encourages affiliates to create good content to help attract and give value to prospective customers. This will also help in avoiding the Google search hammer as Google prefers audience-focused, high-quality authority websites with helpful content as compared to niche sites.

What this means is that instead of making a low-quality niche website or a blog that is filled with a lot of product reviews, it is better to focus on building a high-quality authority website that is filled with solution oriented content.

There are also tools you can use to search for outranked keywords relevant to your topic. These tools will help to give you an insight into what content people are searching for so you can tailor your write-up to match the correct keywords. One free tool that is available to you is the Google search bar.

The Google search bar has a feature called Google Instant.

This feature is what seems to want to help you finish your sentence when typing into the search bar. These suggestions that Google offers should definitely be used in choosing the right topics.

Write Beautiful Articles: Writing is pretty easy. You don't have to be a great writer or word Smith to produce good articles. Most people visiting your website come to your website to be educated, entertained or inspired. Your writing doesn't have to be formal, it can even be casual. Sometimes, you will see that casual writing will outperform formal writing. It doesn't take a genius to write great content and most people are only searching for your experience on the subject matter. So write freely!

Link to Products: Find the product you want to promote on Amazon, you will find a picture and link to the product. It is this link that you put on your articles that are promoting products on your website. You need learn the art of placing links in articles and ensure that they are not out of place while still using relevant hyperlinks.

How Money is Made

If someone follows your recommendation and clicks on your link, they are taken to the Amazon product's page. You get credit for any purchases made within 24 hours. If the customers place some items in their cart, you will get a credit if they purchase those items within 90 days.

You will earn a 4% commission for any sale at the start but if you make more sales, they can raise the commission to 10%. Depending on the number of people who make sales through your affiliate link, you can earn a lot of money. This is the reason why you should continuously be looking for new ways to promote your website.

CHAPTER 23 – DROP SHIPPING

The online business that brings in a ton of money for people all across the globe is drop shipping. Drop shipping accounts for a large chunk of the over $220 billion retail ecommerce market currently in 2017 and this number is expected to rise in the coming years.

Drop shipping is a service offered by wholesalers seeking to expand their market. In drop shipping, you are acting as a retailer for certain products. You do not own the inventory or warehouse and do not have to spend money prior to a sale of any of these products. The products are held by the wholesaler and whenever you have a sale, the wholesaler ships the product to your customer. Take a look at this scenario to help you better understand what drop shipping is about.

In drop shipping, you don't have to worry about the logistics of stocking and the delivery of products. All you concern yourself with is the marketing of your own sales platform and profit margins.

The process of drop shipping is simplified and further explained below.

(1) The customer pays you for the product.

(2) You pay the supplier to send the package.

(3) The supplier sends the product to the customer.

The beauty of drop shipping is the fact that it requires very little capital to setup and get started. You have a large number of wholesalers available who are offering drop shipping services and a wide variety of products to choose from, so all you have to do is create the right sales platform and market it across your entire network.

Drop shipping as a business and marketing strategy is constantly evolving and reaffirming its stand. It's a double win situation for all the parties involved, even though there are few challenges like any other business, but that is what this guide is meant to address. You will find out in the course of reading, the benefits of drop shipping, how to get engaged in drop shipping, the challenges and ways to mitigate them.

Getting Started

It is important you understand if drop shipping is right for you. Does it align with your vision, and goals? Is it something you will be comfortable doing? Do you have the setup readily available, as well as what you need and services you may require? If you can answer these questions in the affirmative, then I think you can proceed.

Drop shipping is not easy money. There is a lot of work to do. You have to have a sales platform, probably a website or blog that is constantly managed and promoted. There may be a need for investment in targeted advertising through major social media platforms such as Facebook.

You will get paid a margin as people purchase the products through you. However, sometimes you may get complaints from customers who become impatient with their orders. In many cases, it will take 2-3 weeks for a product to be drop shipped from your supplier. If your supplier is from an overseas country such as China, this is especially true.

How to become a Drop Shipper

Select the type of products: Decide whether you want to sell products from the fashion, health and fitness, beauty, sporting, collectibles, books or any other business area.

Find Suppliers/Wholesalers: As is the case with most industries, you need to find quality suppliers/wholesalers. Your supplier's product quality is very crucial to your success as drop shippers. You want to check both offline and online to get a good idea of what kind of vendors are out there.

There are various ways to find suppliers willing to offer drop shipping service. The first place I would ask you to look is around you. Find local businesses that offer premium quality products and are willing to expand their market. Approach them, strike a deal so that you get a profit margin from sales, then you can go ahead to market their products on your sales platform. The businesses don't have to be so sophisticated; the local bakery that makes such great cupcakes is a good example of a potential supplier.

The good news is there are a lot of places online that offer such services. Websites like Oberlo, Donald, Ali Express and Worldwide Brands have become very popular in the drop shipping business and presently have tailored solutions for entrepreneurs looking to start their own stores.

The key to finding great suppliers is to filter through many suppliers to get to the right one. Ali Express specifically has some features you can check off including reviews and supplier reliability. When you search for something, on the left hand side of the website search page, you will see the different brands and designs available to you. You can filter and often find products that are selling for a very good price.

Choose a Product that is in demand: When most people think of drop shipping, they think of it as more of a middle man kind of business where they have absolutely no input in the process but to just sit back and promote. True! That may be the case if the ecosystem was not filled with a lot of competition. Research extensively and come up with products that are hot in the market and also try to find unique products that are not being sold by many drop shippers but are still in demand. You can check Google Trends to get an idea of what is in demand and what is not.

To better succeed, you should think of ways to add value. Let's consider an example. You finally decided to launch a business in the fashion niche and you are now selling tailored suits. One of the ways you can add value is to provide scale charts on how to decide on the right kind of suit depending on the body structure. You could also offer a guide on the choice of material or how to match accessories with the suits available.

This may seem trivial to some people but it is of great importance to the customer. Just imagine the number of people whose buying decisions would be based on the information you provide. Whatever value added service you decide to offer, try all you can to make sure that you are providing a great experience for your customers. A customer-first mindset will grow any business.

Design a Sales Platform: This is where all of your marketing efforts will converge. It is on this platform that customers will see the products you are offering. You will see your pending requests, sales options and order management options. Depending on your scale and financial prowess, there are a lot of options to choose from; you can start small and later move on to bigger platforms once you are more comfortable.

Two widely used platforms for people looking to start small include Facebook and Pinterest. You start by creating accounts for your drop shipping business and then promote your products on those platforms and others. The only limitation here is that there may not be any automated payment options but that can be resolved in another way. You can have customers pay directly into your account and proceed to have your suppliers ship products to them.

The more standard way is to take advantage of platforms like Shopify and Oberlo. They both have a great system that is specifically tailored for those involved in the drop shipping atmosphere. To get your online store, all you need to do is to sign up on Shopify or Oberlo by providing basic information such as name, address, etc. They will help you build and launch your own drop shipping website from A-Z with no technical hassles. There is customer support so you should not hesitate to call them if you need help.

Shopify offers a free trial for new drop shippers. Because Shopify has its own features and benefits, it has its own dedicated chapter in this book. You can read more about it there.

CHAPTER 24 - RESEARCH ASSISTANT

The internet is a huge resource for information and has given rise to various online job opportunities. Being an online Research Assistant is one of these beautiful opportunities, it gives you the flexibility of working from your comfort zone in front of your computer. An online Research Assistant is a person who works remotely and provides research reports on various subjects depending on what the client needs. Completed jobs are shared via email, online reports or file sharing solutions.

Individuals and Companies hire Research Assistants for different reasons. It could be because they need someone to search the internet for a piece of information, perform market analysis, conduct telemarketing, do data entry, or use social media to find new markets for products.

To be a successful online Research Assistant, you need some form of experience and coaching. There are platforms like AsssistU.com that offer coaching to aspiring researchers. Login to their website and find out what they are offering and what program best suits your needs.

Getting Started

Research is a very broad subject and it requires specialist knowledge. It is best if you choose an area in which you have already have some prior experience. Your academic background can also help to narrow down a field.

There are a few things you need to know to be successful as a Research Assistant. Your people skills must be great. You should be able to communicate fluently and have great writing and reading skills.

To find work, there are several places available on the web. Look out for Research opportunities on job boards such as Indeed and Monster. You should also join freelance platforms like Wonder, Upwork, Fiverr and People per Hour. There is a constant flow of people looking for online researchers on these platforms so you have the opportunity to work remotely.

These platforms protect you from fraudulent people who may be looking to take advantage of your services but not willing to pay the price. The platforms mentioned above act as an escrow intermediate until the buyer is satisfied with the delivered product.

How much do Research Assistants Earn

For an hourly rate, you could earn as much as $20-$40, but this depends on how much experience you have within a particular niche. If you are just starting off, you would need to build a portfolio with positive ratings; this gives potential clients an impression that you can handle jobs without challenges. Try setting a good rate, your pricing should not compete with those who have been around much longer than you and have built a client base. You should start off with a fair price that is not too high and not too low. You should gradually grow your portfolio and when you have gotten some good ratings; you can then increase the price.

How to Become a Successful Online Research Assistant.

There are a few steps you need to take before you can earn by conducting online research for clients.

Get some Training

An online Research Assistant should have a wide range of

skills on demand. It helps to broaden your range of offers. Initially, your experience will help to reduce the time it takes to turn out reports as you will not be able to outsource the projects. Later on, when you have lots of ratings and are getting lots of orders, you can begin to outsource your projects and turn this venture into passive income.

Choose an area and Create your Profile

Focus on your strengths and knowledgebase. You might have previous experience working as a leads generator or market analyst. When now working as an online research assistant, you can cover topics relating to sales, sales leads, market analysis, brand acceptance, market entry and brand awareness.

You will then need to create your profile, write a catchy bio, create gigs on the kind of services you offer and bid for jobs. You should have a call to action proposal for bidding, which can spark the interest of a client faster. Landing your first client is usually the most difficult, but once you do, the numbers will continue to grow. You can also search for jobs using job boards like Craigslist, Kijiji and LinkedIn.

Network with Other Research Assistants

As much as you can, look for people offering the same service or something similar to what you offer, people who are either working remotely just like you or have an offline day job. Being around these people helps you to learn faster about the job, its challenges, clientele and how to manage them. It is most likely that someone who has far more experience than you should have a lot of tips and tricks on how to be successful within your niche. It will save you time and prevent you from making some costly mistakes or learning the ropes the hard way.

Get your First Job

After you get your first job, give it your best shot, deliver beyond your client's expectation and encourage your client to leave a positive review, as it becomes easier for other people to want to try you out. Happy client, happy seller, everyone is happy.

What are you waiting for, you have an Internet connection, a laptop, a smartphone, you have some idle time, it's time to do some research for someone somewhere who needs it badly. Make the move; you will be glad that you did. Eventually this buiness can become a form of passive income, because you will be able to hire others to do the work for you.

CHAPTER 25 - CONTENT PROVIDER

Do you have a flair for writing or a love for design? Maybe you are already a writer? There is an avenue to harness your skills to make money online. Ever wonder how those beautiful looking websites and blogs are able to turn out creative and valuable content day in and day out that seems to be nonstop?

News and fashion magazines seem to find out about the happenings of the latest trends very quickly. How are they able to write and deliver insightful content that is creative and can stand as authority in the given area?

Most of the contents of blogs, websites and news articles are written by content providers like you and me. Content providing is a tad different from ghostwriting in that content provision involves writing short pieces such as articles, blog posts or the contents on a website, whereas ghostwriting involves a large body of published books.

So how does someone become a content provider? You have to first have a flair for writing video or illustration. Illustration is in high demand right now, and this type of content is actually tailored to those with a flair for design.

Getting started

There are a lot of benefits to providing content. Aside from the monetary benefits, you can also get recognition if the platform you are writing for has a name in the industry. There are various ways to provide content to platforms and depending on your niche and skills, you can find work in any of the categories I will show you below.

Reviews: Your talent may be required in writing reviews. There are lots of niche websites or blogs that need content to keep the users engaged. This is where you come in. if you have experience in that niche or can provide reviews for products; you've got yourself a job.

Newsletters/e-zines: Lots of online newsletters now require content providers to regularly provide trending and insightful content to be published on their website. Publishers of e-zines and online newsletters are looking for content providers that can engage users and have them coming back for more.

Opinion columns: These are online newsletters that reflect the writer's personal opinion. There are platforms that are seeking your voice on their news articles or newsletters. You may be required to turn out provocative write-ups that elicit a conversation or have the readers coming back for more.

Traditional articles: These are regular articles that you find on blogs and websites. They are usually just centered on a subject and they require you to share your expert knowledge and experience. Some research may be required.

Illustrations: if you are graphically inclined, there are comic websites that need your short illustrated stories for publishing. Because of the large market and the demand from the enthusiasts, regular content is needed to meet the demand. Your short illustrated stories could possibly sell for a premium here.

How to succeed as a Content Provider

There are skills and practice that are required to succeed at content providing. You will need to show a lot of professionalism on the job, ensure that the write ups are properly proofread and checked for plagiarism. Some large websites have the capacity to employ editors who will run checks for them. Other tools are available on the internet such as Grammarly and Copyscape. Keep them handy and use them regularly. Below are a few skills you should have.

Prompt Delivery: This is a fast paced industry, so you have to deliver quickly. The rate at which you can produce quality write ups is bound to set you apart from the competition. Website owners and publishers are looking for content providers who can deliver quality within a good time frame.

Self-Editing: This is one skill that you should develop if you are going to continue for long in this industry. There are lots of online software that can help with editing but because they are automated, they are not perfect, so your skill and knowledge of editing will help fill in the gaps created by software editors.

Marketing Skills: You should possess a good working knowledge of business, contract negotiation and management. You need to have the ability to discern a good offer from a bad one. Some offers would have you writing but not making any money. Avoid such offers especially when you are not getting anything such as recognition in return. Your writing is a business, treat it as such. If you can, request for an advance payment. I have seen instances where the client refused to make payment after the work had been completed. Ensure that a contract is signed for large orders, as it protects both parties.

Promote Your Craft

There are several ways you can promote your craft and find jobs. There are a lot of jobs for content providers just as there are lots of content providers. You have to set yourself apart from the rest by following these few tips before and when promoting your craft. These tips will greatly improve your craft and help yousell your skill.

Create a portfolio: Most website owners and publishers want to see samples of work that you have previously done before committing to a contract. It is important to have a portfolio that can be viewed online because it will show your professionalism and preparation. Arrange and manage it for easy navigation. You can host a portfolio on your website or on web platforms like Format, which caters to designers and illustrators; or Wix and WordPress, which are geared towards all kinds of content providers.

In creating and publishing your works, be mindful of NDA's (Non-Disclosure Agreements) so that you are legally protected. For published works that were written by you, you would do well to convert all writing samples to .jpg (images). This will help you to avoid issues with plagiarism. Lastly, have a resume handy to send to clients. Your portfolio should usually have a profile in it, which can be sent via email at the click of a button.

Find Jobs

There are several avenues to find work as a content provider. Online platforms like Craigslist have ads that are constantly running and are updated daily by people who are seeking the services of content providers. Here you will find copywriting, web content and guest posting jobs that you can check out.

One other good way to get jobs is through referrals. Those you have worked for previously are in great standing to helping you get other jobs if they were satisfied with your previous work. It is good to develop a good working relationship with those you work for to ensure that whenever there is an opportunity, your name is the first one that comes to mind.

You could also reach out to website owners via email or social media, asking for an opportunity to guest post on their platforms. Send them your resume and a link to your portfolio for consideration. On social media, little things like making insightful posts or running creative commentaries can land you jobs. Use your profile as a marketing channel for your craft. Write short articles and drop links to your portfolio showing the documents that have been published. Share your post and ask others to do same.

Finally, advertise. You can pay for advertisements on platforms like Facebook, or on social forums where you know you are likely to get clients from. Be socially active, interact, create connections and you will succeed.

CHAPTER 26 - ONLINE LEAD GENERATION

Online lead generation is the holy grail of online businesses. People can sometimes find something they fancy in the course of reading or browsing the internet, and make a call to inquire about it. It could also be that they take part in a survey that is aimed at capturing their opinion on a particular subject.

What these actions mean to you as a marketing guru is what is called a lead. These customers have given you an insight into what their preferences and concerns are about your business or service. On this basis, you can open communication with them on how you can better offer service or products without it seeming like a cold call. Because there was a prior connection between your business and the individual, you can reach out to them to offer services or products that are tailored to their needs.

Lead generation is the process of finding unique ways to convert potential customers into buyers. It is about finding ways to get customers from people who have shown an interest in your service or products through methods such as filling out surveys or contact forms. Because several people may have shown interest in your client's product or service, there is a need to understand and qualify those who can be called leads.

Getting started

Generally speaking, a sales lead is simply the gathering of information. The amount of information you can collect from an individual is key to helping you decide if that individual can be termed a lead or not. There are several methods to ensure that the individual provides as much information as possible so you can make the correct decision.

Let's say you're offering a free service, but before individuals can get such a service, they need to register by providing their details such as name, email, address and any other information that you may deem necessary. The information provided by the user on the form he or she has filled will give you an insight on how to tailor your offerings to meet the customer's needs. Essentially, this is lead generation.

As an online lead generator for small businesses, your responsibility is to fashion out a lead generation strategy and attract the right customers. The components of a winning lead generation strategy are outlined below.

Visitor: he or she has been discovered through one of your marketing channels e.g. website, blog or feed.

Call to Action (CTA): This is usually an image or button on your channel that asks the visitor to perform an action. This image or button then redirects them to your landing page.

Landing page: this is where the user is redirected to after clicking the call to action. It can be used for a variety of purposes, one of which is to capture leads.

Forms: this can be found on the landing page and it is used to collect user information in exchange for an offer.

Offer: it must have substance and be valuable enough to allow the user to share information with you.

Tips to becoming a successful lead generator

In generating leads, data is important. It is generated data that tells you how well your strategies are working and where to channel your resources. A good lead generator must understand the methods of developing strategy, what to look out for, and how to implement actionable plans for the success of this strategy. I will be showing you a few tips on how you can put together a successful lead generation campaign.

Lead Generation Tools

Using the right lead generation tool is going to greatly impact your campaign. These tools help you analyze your web traffic and provide statistics about people that are visiting your sales channel and the actions they are performing. This allows you to have enough information to make planning easier. Without this information, it becomes difficult to fully ascertain your sales position and planning is almost impossible.

There are a few templates and tools out there that make the task easier. Tools like CTA Templates provide free clickable CTA buttons to embed on your website. There are several others, and you can browse the internet to find out about them.

Create Amazing Offers

Create valuable content. As you build the sales channel (website or blog), let the user be offered a valuable experience and with it, you can create CTA. Remember to insert CTA in the content. This could encourage the user to claim a prize, or to learn more, or to take part in an offer. Just create as many offers as you can to attract the user and make them available for profiling. At whatever stage a customer is in the buying cycle, your CTA should be able to tell and offer clicks that fit the user. This is why it is important to use a smart CTA. Smart CTA's are able to tell where a user is in the buying cycle. They can tell you whether someone is a new user, a potential lead or a customer.

Have a Dedicated Landing Page

It is good practice to link your CTA to a dedicated landing page. I have seen instances where CTA's have directed me to the homepage of the targeted website. I am now left with the option of navigating the website to find the offer or I just quit and close the web page. To avoid this, it is important that you create a dedicated landing page for all your offers. Whatever offer that a CTA is linked to should have its own page.

It is no use getting visitors to click only to lose them due to negligence. Create a page that converts visitors into leads.

Use Social Media

Social media is very important in any promotional campaign. Adopt a link-dropping strategy on your social profiles; this is a situation where you create CTA's on your profiles on Facebook, Instagram or Twitter that redirect to a landing page. It is good practice to inform the visitor that they will be redirected out of the page they are in at the moment.

This is a cheap and very effective way to generate a lead. It has proven to be very successful. The key is to create visually appealing CTA that truly attracts the users and it should be backed with an offer to encourage them to make the move. For effective channel utilization, you can perform a lead generation analysis to help you ascertain which posts or articles have generated the most leads and create links to them in other posts or articles.

Engage your followers by creating a contest where a winner gets a prize to encourage activity on your profile that can lead to a lead. Facebook has a feature that allows you to put a simple call to action button at the top of your page to encourage users to take action and be redirected straight to your website or blog. Also, there is a twitter lead generator card that helps you to generate leads within a tweet without having to leave twitter.

Find Customers

Now that you know how to create CTA and how leads are generated, it is time to promote yourself. Firstly though, you should be aware that you will also need to update your knowledge regularly. There are tools and templates but that's not enough. It will be in your best interest to also do a bit of more research on tools that will be beneficial to helping you grow your business and service.

As a lead generator for small businesses, you can use these same methods I have talked about to aggregate the promotion of your service. Create a website, utilize social media, let potential customers see that you can generate leads for their business the same way they became leads for the business.

CHAPTER 27 - 3D ANIMATION AND MODELLING

Are you creative? What's your impression of animated films and videos? Like me, I believe you were also a fan of cartoons way back. What about those superheroes and Marvel comics? You might be wondering my reasons for asking these questions but I need you to transport yourself, like the Transformers, into the world of animation.

Animations have been a part of our lives since the days of Walt Disney's Mickey Mouse. The practice, although old, is still an integral part of our lives and the process has now transformed into something so much better, namely 3D animation.

Unlike your old 2D animations, 3D animations make use of special software to create a three-dimensional moving, digital image. These images are applied in film production, product modeling, marketing and promotions. Opportunities to earn money are plentiful, all you need is the required skill set, a computer with the 3D animation software installed and a flair to model and animate characters.

Getting Started

To earn a living from 3D animation and modeling, you will need to dedicate time and effort to the art. Because it is a process that involves creativity, it would require your utmost attention when creating models. The amount of effort you devote to it, and the tools at your disposal, will ultimately determine how well you will perform in this line of work.

Before starting out, it is advisable you consider if this work is suitable to your persona. Certain skill sets and prerequisite knowledge is necessary to perform excellently, but if you do not possess these, what you lack in them can be made up by flair and interest.

How to Become a Professional 3D Animator

When becoming a professional animator, you need to choose the right software, decide on your niche and find your market.

Choosing the Right Software

For 3D animation, different software serve different purposes. The most common software available for 3D animation include Autodesk 3DS Max, Autodesk Maya and Blender. Your choice of software should reflect your intent. By intent I mean your niche as each one has its advantages and limitations. Let us examine the software below.

Autodesk 3DS Max: This is the leading 3D software for gaming. It is one of the most widely used software for achieving three-dimensional digital imagery.

Autodesk Maya: This is the most popular software. It is widely used in creating visual effects for movies. It is the industry standard, highly scalable and very flexible.

Blender: This software is free. It has gained lots of attention for its small size, flexibility and scalability. It is the usual choice for newbies and offers a range of possibilities for visual effects in gaming and video editing for both small and large scale projects.

Deciding on Your Niche

There are quite a number of areas to specialize in this business. The better an authority you are in a particular area, the more likely you'll earn more. There are several ways you can define your niche.

You can decide on only making stock models. A stock model is a physical 3D model of an object, scene, or scenario. This is quite a profitable niche and is usually for the more accomplished animator, but nothing should stop you from trying it out. Unleash your creativity; make as many models as possible and sell them to other designers who may need them for ongoing or future projects.

There are several places to fit into and find your market. You can choose visual effects for gaming, film or both. Choose what appeals to you and also what has demand in the market. This will help you become an authority quickly. You may also research the necessary skillset you will need to develop in order to be successful in the area you choose.

Film: This is a potent field for 3D animators. Your skill can be used to produce short animated skits or films, which can be used for marketing campaigns by companies to sell an idea or to simply entertain people. Your services can also be harnessed in the mainstream movie industry. If you are extraordinary, you can approach studios to outsource their visual effects to you, which is almost always cheaper than hiring a standby animator.

Gaming: With the advent of app development, the opportunities for small gaming companies are on the rise. From the comfort of your living room, you can create and publish your own gaming app. This is a great way to harness your skill. The benefits are enormous because should your app become popular, you may just be on your way to becoming a millionaire.

Educational Illustrations: This made the cut because I

realized that on forums and job boards, there are a lot of folks making money using Blender for illustrations. They are mainly targeting the authors of children books. There are many people who are creating illustrations and selling them to authors, who in turn publish their books on Amazon.

Finding a Market

One of the most potent ways of finding a ready market for your models is to check freelance platforms and job boards. There are several freelance platforms that cater exclusively to visual artists, including animators. Platforms like VideoToOrder.com cater exclusively to visual artists. Other platforms like Fiverr.com, Upwork.com and Freelancer.com all have animations as part of their gigs. Craigslist is also a very good job board for marketing, not just your skill but also your models.

Instagram, Facebook, Vimeo; these are all hotbeds for showcasing your talent. Work on growing your followership. The truth is that if your work is great and unique, you shouldn't find it difficult to grow a large following in a short time.

Blender also operates an e-shop where works produced using their software can be displayed for sale. Various items can be put up for sale on the e-shop including educational materials and 3D models. The key to succeeding here is to be unique and to pay good attention to detail. Amazon is also a great marketplace for you. They recently launched the Amazon Video Direct (AVD) program, where you can create your store and upload things to be sold on this platform.

Finally there is YouTube. This is the world's largest video publishing site as YouTube gets millions of visitors daily. I would advise you to create a channel here and let it serve as a hotbed where you display your creativity for all to see. And in time, when you have grown a large subscriber list, you can further monetize it to improve your earnings.

Marketing and Promotions

I have covered a bit on how to find a market for your skill in the previous section but I just want to reiterate it here. To get the best potential out of your knowledge, it is important that you diversify your marketing and promotion strategy. Having a website is great but it is important that you are seen on platforms where you don't have to worry about driving traffic, and terms like "keywords" and "meta tag."

Instagram is a good place to start your marketing and promotion campaign. Creating an account is free and you are allowed up to one minute of video uploads. It is advised that you make great use of this medium so that you can publish content that promotes your work.

Facebook is the largest social network. Having a defined presence here would help your brand. Create an account or page exclusively for your work and publish creative content. Share it with a friend and ask them to share it too. Just continue to push for visibility and it will pay off in no time. If you have a bit of extra money, you can invest in Facebook advertising. It has proven to be a wise investment for many who have done it.

Be active on discussion boards and forums relating to 3D animation. This creates an opportunity for collaboration. Relationships formed here could be the push you to your desired platform.

Keep doing that and you will only get better at it.

CHAPTER 28 - SOCIAL MEDIA INFLUENCER

In this age of social media, there are a few roles that have been erected and these roles serve as rallying points in this online space. One of the roles that has become popular in recent years is the social media influencer.

Defining a social media influencer is as straightforward as it sounds. We can refer to a social media influencer as a person who has a very large following on the various social media platforms and exerts a measure of control over his or her followers. By virtue of who they are, they can influence the buying decision and the thoughts of a lot of their followers. Celebrities, sports stars, actors, politicians and leaders all fit this bill.

You fall under the latter group. You see, I am guessing that you are not a celebrity, a sports star, an actor or a politician. We want to grow our following as normal people and if we become social media "celebrities" in the process, that is just a bonus.

Social media sites have become a rallying point for a lot of people, especially from the younger age group. These individuals span different niches including gaming, fashion, sports, comedy and information technologyy. These people are not celebrities in the real world, but in the online realm they are kings and queens.

Who is a Social Media Influencer?

Social media influencers are passionate people. It was their passion that made them popular. They stand for an idea and express their passion. Some are great teachers, others are inspirational speakers and some are fashion experts. One thing they all have in common is passion.

In business, a social media influencer is someone who uses his or her influence to promote a particular brand, service or interest to his or her followers and can convert them to customers for the respective brand or company.

How Do Social Media Influencers Earn?

Social media influencers are one of the biggest earners in the world today. A majority of their income comes from branding. Earnings for social media influencers vary a lot. There are no fixed amounts but their following, to large extent, determines how much they can earn. Also, the client's budget and marketing objectives also make a difference.

Brand Rep/Ambassador: Social media influencers can monetize themselves by taking advantage of their popularity to become brand ambassadors or representatives for major brands.

Sell Digital Products: They can use their influence and sell digital products such as ebooks, how-to courses, or videos. Fitness queen Kayla Itsines is a great example of this. She has been able to make and sell her workout program and her newly launched app "Sweat with Kayla."

Make Sponsored Posts: In this case, you can use your profile as a potent advertisement tool. Make sponsored posts for brands and companies for a one-time fee.

Physical Products: You can sell physical products. Even when you don't manufacture anything, you can sell other brands' products through your profile. Makeup artist and YouTube channel owner Jaclyn Hill's collaboration with cosmetics brand Becca is a good example of this.

Affiliate Marketing: One way you can take advantage of your followers is by becoming an affiliate marketer. Affiliate marketers have the medium to reach millions of people and earn well for themselves.

How to be Successful as a Social Media Influencer

There are certain practices that will put you ahead in being a successful social media influencer. But first, your personality must be built on trust. Any untrue aspect about yourself should be disclosed upfront, if not it will come out when you start becoming popular.

Build a Following: The easiest way most social media influencers have come to prominence is through their content. They all have great content that suits their niche. Creative content is the major elixir. Even if you invest in driving traffic and advertising, if you do not have good content, you will lose the following after a short while. It is great content that encourages a user to follow and invite others to do same.

An investment in growing your following is not a bad idea especially since you are just starting out. Organically growing followers these days is very difficult. So, you have to act wisely to invest in boosting your following. There are agencies and freelancers who would do this for you for a small fee.

CHAPTER 29 - ONLINE BRAND STRATEGIST

An online brand strategist is one whose responsibilities have a controlling interest in the online reaches of the brand he or she represents. Brand strategists organize strategies and implement digital promotions of the brand with the aim of getting them the needed visibility.

Online brand strategists will find ways to further enhance the branding of a product or service, as well as develop a marketing plan through the analysis of current data and trends. They are expected to implement strategies in line with their findings in order to better achieve visibility for the clients. The brand strategist will do well if he or she is familiar with statistics and research analysis.

Is This Role Right for You?

The online brand strategist is expected to cater to small businesses looking to coalesce their offline and online marketing strategy, or to help large brands who are looking to push new products into the online space through their new campaign strategies.

The skills required to perform exceptionally in this job are:

1.   Emotional intelligence

2.   Statistical and analytical skills

3.   Ability to interpret large data

4.   Content marketing skills

5.   Social media advertising skills

How Much Does an Online Brand Strategist Earn?

According to PayScale.com, a brand strategist earns an average salary of $66,384. But that is as a salaried strategist. As an *online* brand strategist your earning abilities are greatly affected by your client's budget, the scope of work you will receive, your skill set and your bargaining power.

How to Become a Successful Online Brand Strategist

The online brand strategist is expected to build a strategy around the marketing objective of his client. There are no specific skills required but going by the job requirements, an online brand strategist should be a good reader, writer, communicator, he or she should have emotional intelligence, know how to interpret large data, and have social advertising skills. The online brand strategist should be a deadline-conscious person.

Research: It is important that you are up to date on happenings around your client's business. What is the latest trend? Who is creating buzz? What is the competition doing? What are the influences on the market? All of these are pertinent questions that you should be able to ask yourself. Research these and come up with strategies that can help drive your client's brand to the next level. Social media is a good place to start.

To create strategies that can convert users, you have to have information. Invest in research, ask the right questions, and come up with great strategy. Read books, read journals and reports, and invest in tools to monitor trends. All of these habits will help you perform better as an online brand strategist.

CHAPTER 30 - YOUTUBE VIDEOS

YouTube is the world's largest video publishing website, it has over 300 hours of video downloaded every minute and over 5 billion videos watched in a single day. This should give you an insight into the size of this video publishing platform.

There is so much opportunity to make money from YouTube and the purpose of this guide is to show you how you can take advantage of this great platform to benefit yourself.

Before I proceed, I would like to ask you, what is your passion? The main thrust of making money on YouTube is passion. Without passion, you can't keep going. Outside of the Search Engine Optimization (SEO) or the marketing strategies, it is the passion that shows through and is the most important factor.

Your passion is reflected in your content and content is king! Let me break down this idea a little:

Imagine the number of videos that exist and think about what the motivation would be for someone to watch your videos? There is absolutely no motivation. The only driving force that would make someone want to see your video is CONTENT!

There are two main ways to making money on YouTube:

1.   Great content

2.   Large following

Without great content, all marketing strategies, implementation, and resultant success will go to waste as the traffic gained will eventually be lost due to poor content.

Without adequate traffic, there is no way you can monetize your channel. YouTube has recently updated their AdSense policy. The updated policy stipulates that only channels with over 10,000 views are eligible for AdSense.

How do You Make Money?

There are 3 major ways channel owners can make money from YouTube:

1. Affiliate marketing

2. Google AdSense

3. From FANS

Getting Started

Building your YouTube channel's reputation and viewership to the level where you are making money from Google AdSense will definitely take a while. You need to grow your followership enough to benefit from Google AdSense and that means putting in lots of effort, but you can explore other streams of revenue from your YouTube channel. The goal is that you develop a great idea by creating quality content.

Idea

Your central idea is the major factor that will decide your content. Being comfortable with what you do and are willing to share with the world is important. Many YouTube channel owners make money by sharing their daily life experiences while others show the steps involved in performing specific activities.

Let your idea speak to your audience. This is what will have them coming back every day. Let the content you share be one that is witty and catchy. Your content should be designed so that it attracts new followers and retains loyalty from existing followers.

Winning Followers

There are many strategies that you can apply to growing your YouTube subscriber list. The strategies I will share with you are effective and have been used by some of the leading YouTube channel owners online. You will be starting out a step ahead as a professional. The strategy is a 9 point strategy:

1.   Create a custom thumbnail

2.   Have catchy titles

3.   Implement keywords that match videos in search results

4.   Infuse a call-to-action

5.   Make your video easy to embed

6.   Cross promote your YouTube channel

7.   Make playlists

8.   Be consistent

9.   Engage your viewers (contests, response videos and collaborations)

1. Create a custom thumbnail

The attention span of the average viewer is less than 2.5 seconds, so you only have a few seconds to capture the attention of the viewer. The catchier you're video's title and thumbnail, the better the chance of someone clicking on your video.

Let your thumbnail image reflect your ideology. The thumbnail is the image that is shown when your video appears in a search, or when it is embedded on another platform.

The size of your custom thumbnail is important.

Google recommends that your thumbnail should be:

Size: 1280X720 (minimum width of 640 pixels) 2MB limit

Formats: .JPG, .GIF, .BMP, or .PNG.

16:9 aspect ratio.

You can upload a custom thumbnail as soon as you upload a video by simply choosing the custom thumbnail option.

2. Let your title sell

Let your title be catchy, but don't let it get away from the message. Your title should tell viewers in short words what the content or idea of your video is going to be about. You need to make it sound exciting and try to include keywords for better SEO.

3. Keywords for SEO

There are several different YouTube optimization techniques that can improve your search rankings, but the most important of them all is keyword research. The main point here is to focus on keyword searches in Google that will almost always turn up video results.

For instance, if someone searches Google for "slow dancing," it is only natural that Google would turn up a results page full of videos, simply because dancing is something most people would want to see than read about.

If you find a lot of video results instead of just text listings on the first page then that keyword should be what you would want to align your tags with. But you can also interplay the word with something similar to it, and if it still calls up videos in searches then that is what you should use to avoid stiff competition. It may sound like a mouthful right now but with practice you will get better at it.

4. Infuse a call-to-action to engage viewers

A call to action is a user engagement tool that implores the user to perform an action during and at the end of your video. Call-to-actions are very important marketing tools. YouTube categorizes user action into 4 groups: watch more videos, like and share, leave a comment, and subscribe to the channel. You are advised to infuse one or more of these call-to-actions during your video or at end of your video. The tactics also include:

Direct Host-Mentions: This is where you directly ask the viewer politely to perform an action. It could range from leaving a comment to subscribing to the channel.

End-cards: This is another beautiful way to infuse a call-to-action. In this method, a card appears at the end of the video asking the user to perform an action like subscribing to the channel. This card should be clickable and make the process seamless.

Video Descriptions: Video descriptions are important. In describing your videos, make use of your keywords like we have described above. Put a link to your website or your social media accounts in your description. This will make you more accessible and provide opportunities for further engagement.

5. Make it easy for people to embed your videos

When uploading videos to your YouTube channel, you have the option to decide on embedding. The embed feature allows people to publish your video on their website or blog. This is a fantastic way to gain more visibility.

A viewer can copy and paste the link that appears when they click share on your video to embed it. The more shares you get the better.

6. Cross-promote your YouTube channel:

Be consistent about it. Always infuse you videos into other platforms you manage and promote them on those platforms. Sites where you can cross promote include your social media accounts, emails and newsletters. Find ways to make your videos relevant to all your other content to leverage those eyeballs.

7. Make playlists

There are lots of reasons to group your videos into playlists. Playlists make your videos easier to find and they can also help with search rankings.

The beautiful thing about playlists is that they ensure the next video on your list gets to play without viewer input when it is set to auto-play. There is a trick you can explore here. Make a playlist and include videos that are popular in your niche, that way they will come up in searches. Playlists also give you an opportunity to associate your videos with keywords for better SEO. The playlist description can associate new keywords with your videos and open up new search opportunities.

8. Create a weekly video series

This is one of the best ways to encourage users to subscribe. If you are creating content that is witty the users will know when you make updates and come back. They will more than likely subscribe to your channel. This also allows you to feature your other videos to your users. This could be a Friday series or a top of the week one. Whatever works for you will do just fine.

9. Engage your viewers

Create contests and games to engage your users. Collaborate with other brands to liven up your channel. You have to be active on your channel by responding to user's requests, demands, or questions. This is a social platform so that means you need to engage in real time, be relevant and genuine. Encourage feedback, gauge the responses and engage the viewer. By doing so, you make them loyal. People will keep coming back to your channel. Viewer engagement is very important.

These are just a few tips to get you started. Do not forget to open a PayPal account if you don't have one since that's where your earnings will go into. I hope that you apply these tips and they work for you.

CHAPTER 31 - COMMODITIES TRADING

Commodities trading, like its financial counterpart, is a fairly easy venture to embark upon. Before now, most investors did not consider commodity trading as a viable venture due to the significant amount of time, money and expertise that was required in this field. Today however, there are a number of ways to invest in the commodities market and some of these methods have made it easy for ordinary people and non-professional traders alike to participate in commodity trading.

Commodity trading involves the trade in commodities such as oil, precious metals, agricultural produce or natural resources. In the not too distant past, in order to trade commodities you were required to apply with a broker and wait for him or her to call back. Sometimes the wait could go on forever. Today, there are a number of online options available to trade commodity options.

Getting Started

The trade in commodities requires a bit of knowledge on how the market operates. I will ask that you pay close attention here. There is more than one way to trade commodities online and each method has its own individual risk/reward factor.

How to Invest in Commodities

Futures Contract: This is one of the most popular ways to invest in the commodities market. In this method, there is an agreement to buy or sell a specific quantity of a commodity at a specific price in the future. Futures are available in every category of commodities. The two types of investors who are major participants in this type of trade are the commercial or institutional users of the commodities and the speculators.

Commercial/Institutional Users: This category invests to diversify their portfolio and sometimes for budgetary and planning purposes as well.

Speculators: This is where you fall into. These investors have their sole aim on profits. They are looking to benefit from the fluctuation in the price of the commodity they have invested in. For instance, you make a $50,000 investment in a futures contract for oil because you believe that the price of oil will increase significantly in the near future.

You are required to open an account with any of the reputable brokerage service firms available on the Internet to trade in commodity futures. Depending on your commodity of choice, there is a specific minimum deposit. The futures market trade is similar to the Forex market. You buy into a position and depending on the fluctuation in the price of that commodity; you either make a profit or suffer a loss.

Advantages: There are some advantages with trading futures. One of the major advantages is that you are not actually buying the product, but underplaying the market instead to gain a profit. There is the leverage that allows for big profits if you are on the right side of the trade, and this also allows you to use small amounts to trade in full-size contracts.

Disadvantages: The futures market can be very volatile and investment in these markets is very risky. Leverage magnifies both gains and losses. A trade can go against you quickly, and you could lose your deposit and more in just a short span of time.

Options: Options on futures contracts is a little like placing a deposit rather than an outright purchase. You have the right, but not the obligation, to follow through on the transaction. So, if the price of the contract doesn't move in the direction you anticipate, you have limited your loss to the cost of the option.

Stocks: You invest in the shares of companies trading in the commodities market.

ETF (Exchange Traded Funds): This allows you to trade in the futures market without making any form of direct investment. The scope of this area is a little larger than this guide.

Tips to Becoming a Successful Commodities Trader

Education

This is very important! Just because commodities is easy does not imply that you should neglect acquiring the proper education on how the market operates and how to succeed when trading commodities. Learning about commodities is integral to a trader's success, although the majority of your learning will come from live trading and experience. It is important that you learn everything possible about the Commodities markets, including the geopolitical and economic factors that affect prices. It is also important that you are flexible and ready to adapt to changes in market conditions. Your strategies should reflect your thoughts on the market. I suggest that you test them out first on demo accounts where there is no risk of losing money.

You would be required to regularly update your knowledge and strategies. Constant learning is one of the hallmarks of being a successful trader.

Find a Reputable Broker

There are scams everywhere in this market. Commodities trading is a very profitable venture and it attracts all manner of characters, legit and dubious alike. There are regulatory bodies that perform oversight functions in the industry, and it is advisable that you only do business with brokers that are regulated and licensed by the National Futures Association (NFA) and the U.S. Commodity Futures Trading Commission (CFTC). Countries outside of the US have their own regulatory bodies with which legitimate commodities brokers should register.

There are many brokers on the Internet making mouth-watering offers to aspiring commodities traders. Please research carefully, do your due diligence and take heed of the advice given above. There are a couple of things to look out for when deciding on the right broker for you; look out for their policy on minimum deposits, deposit methods, leverage, spread, withdrawal, minimum withdrawals and withdrawal duration. Compare your findings amongst the competitors to find the legitimate one with the best offer.

A vibrant customer service is a key indicator of a good broker. If they can be reached on multiple channels and respond promptly to inquiries, then it is usually safe to trade with them.

Demo Accounts

One of the key offerings of most major commodities trading platforms is the demo account. In this account, you are given the opportunity to practice trading commodities. It is also on this platform that you can build, test and perfect your strategies. There is no risk on this platform, all trades mirror live trades without the attendant risks.

Experiment on this platform. Practice, then practice some more. Do not move to a real money account until you have mastered the craft. Be patient. Learn all you can and practice on the demo. When you feel you are ready, you can move to the live trades.

Build a Strategy

Learn from successful traders or even from your own practice time. Observe the strategies that have performed well for you and apply those strategies to your live trades. Choose the right indicator and color scheme that suits you. This allows you to monitor the various positions on the market.

Proper money management techniques are required for successful trading. Knowing when to exit a trade is way more important than knowing when to enter. You can make money entering the market at any position. The key is to know when to exit.

Building a successful trading strategy should incorporate good trading knowledge and great money management techniques. Leverage is very high in this market and as such, the possibility for quick profits is high but so is the risk of great loss.

Start Small

Physiological factors like emotions are not fully taken into account in demo trades. Because you are now trading with real money, the physiological impulses come into full effect. A champ on a demo may fail woefully on an introduction to live trades. You have to protect against this by starting out small. Place trades with a small amount,and test your strategies.

Find the strategy that works for you, apply proper money management techniques, and as your trade stabilizes, increase gradually.

Your understanding of leverage is important. Leverage works through ratios, so take for example, a broker offers you a leverage of 100:1. What this means is that if your initial investment is $100, you have the opportunity to place trade positions of up to $10,000. Take heed though, this exposes you to greater risk, so I advise that you use it wisely.

Record Keeping

Keeping records helps you to learn from past trades. Your records should contain dates, instruments, profits, loss and your performance and overall emotional disposition during the trades. This gives insight into your trading patterns and allows you know what to avoid and how to improve. Without a journal, you are likely to make the same mistakes again.

Aside from the benefits of insight, a good record allows you keep track of trades for tax purposes. Discuss with a tax specialist on what is required of you and fulfill them to avoid legal trouble.

Commodities Trading is a Business

Like all businesses geared for profit, you should focus on a strategy that is functional and sustainable. Individual successes do not translate to overall success however. You have to sustain success before concluding that the business is successful. Have a risk absorption plan in place.

And don't get emotional when trading. Set realistic goals and you will go far.

CHAPTER 32 - CRYPTOCURRENCY

When I first heard the word cryptocurrency, I thought it was something out of a comic book, like something to do with Superman. Little did I know that this word would become the new face of financial transactions in the future.

Cryptocurrency trading refers to the trade in all digital currencies. This is an entirely new market. Most brokerage firms are just adopting it as client demand continues to grow. Let's get a brief background on cryptocurrency.

Cryptocurrencies are digital currencies; they were first introduced by a man named Satoshi Nakamoto in 2009. He sought to create a new form of currency that cannot be controlled by any government but derives its value from the acceptability of its users. The currency became widespread across the world. It has continued to grow and is even estimated to becoming a major instrument of worldwide trade.

The first cryptocurrency introduced is called Bitcoin and its unit is the Satoshi. Over the years, other currencies have been developed and are in use. Some of the cryptocurrencies in circulation include Ethereum, Litecoin, and TBC. These are just some of the major cryptocurrencies in circulation.

The trade in cryptocurrency received a boost when major technology giants like Microsoft, IBM and billionaire investors like Warren Buffet adopted it and made large investments into the trade.

Today many merchants accept cryptocurrencies for the exchange of goods and services.

Getting Started

Trading cryptocurrency is no different from trading Forex. The same rules apply but here the currency exchanges are usually between fiat currencies, especially the dollar, and the various cryptocurrencies. There are a few terms you should be aware of:

Wallet: This where you store your coins. Examples include Mycelium, Paxil, etc.

Exchange: These are platforms set up to manage and facilitate the exchange of cryptocurrency.

Blockchain: The platform on which the Bitcoin infrastructure thrives.

To trade in cryptocurrencies, you purchase coins from exchanges or from other traders like yourself. You usually trade fiat currency (dollar) with the cryptocurrency of your choice. The intention of purchasing the coin is in anticipation of a rise in value that can be translated to profit.

Many Forex brokers now offer cryptocurrency as part of their instruments. You can gain more insight on how to operate and trade successfully from the guide on Forex.

Tips to Become a Successful Cryptocurrency Trader

Education

It is very important that you get your knowledge game right. There are free online resources where you can read further on the subject. It is important that you acquire proper education and knowledge on how the market operates and how to succeed in trading cryptocurrencies. Learning about the inner workings of cryptocurrencies and understanding the market is integral to a trader's success. There are several factors such as news, investment paradigms (as was the case with Litecoin recently when they determined the direction of the market). It is also important to have flexibility and to make sure that you can adapt quickly to market fluctuations.

You would be required to update your knowledge on a regular basis as the market is constantly evolving.

Decide on an Exchange

The responsibility of an exchange is to manage trades within the ecosystem. There are several exchange platforms with their individual rules and regulations. In choosing an exchange, it is important that you read and understand their rules and regulations before committing any significant amount of money to trades. Examples of exchanges include Coinbase, Poloniex, Bitfinex, Kraken and Luno.

It is also important to read the reviews and opinions of people on the services offered by the various exchanges before deciding on the one to trade on.

Tools

There are a couple of financial tools that you need to help you make successful forecasts by keeping you up to date on the financial position of the market. These applications are useful for tracking the price of cryptocurrencies on your phone and a lot more.

Blockfolio: The Blockfolio app allows you create a watch list that you can add trades to. This helps you keep track of your portfolio's performance at all times. The currency display feature is one great thing about it because it displays all the currencies on your watch list. Some apps insist on displaying the value in Bitcoin, which can be annoying.

Coincap: Currencies are displayed by market capitalization on Coincap. The cap volume and other ranking factors can be specified by you. They also have cool charts which are quite useful for providing information on what is actively being traded. It also displays prices in your currency of choice.

Build a Strategy

Learn from successful traders the strategies and the tools necessary to your trades as it is important you know what to look out for when trading cryptocurrencies. Take full advantage of spreads.

Choose the right indicator and color scheme that suit you. This allows you to monitor the various positions of the market effectively.

Good money management skills are very important, trade only on established coins like Bitcoin, Litecoin and Ethereum. Run far away from coins advertised as having great prospects for acceptability and growth. This is not to say you should not look out for new prospective markets from which you can cash in on. Just be careful and do your due diligence.

Building a successful trading strategy involves learning from others, incorporating good trading knowledge and great money management techniques.

Conclusion

In spite of the great benefit of cryptocurrencies, it could also be detrimental if approached without the prerequisite knowledge. Avoid the pitfalls of promises and hype.

CHAPTER 33 - ONLINE AUCTION

The Internet has opened a wide range of opportunities for people to interact and engage in business. One of the fastest growing and easy-to-do-from-home businesses is an online auction.

Today, there are lots of platforms offering auction services. Sites like eBay and uBid are two of the world's largest online auction platforms that bring together millions of buyers and sellers. They are examples of perfect platforms for the visibility and marketing of your products.

Auctions are a great way to make money. They afford the seller an opportunity to get maximum value for their commodity. A seller advertises their product, bids are placed, and the highest bid wins. This is simply what auctions are all about. So how do you make money from online auctions?

Online auctions provide a great platform for individuals to earn passive income. Some have gone on to make it a full-time business and are making a lot of money from it. The choice is up to you on whether it's going to be a passive income or a full-time business.

Getting Started

To make money from online auctions, it will require a great deal of creativity from you. You would have to decide on what you will be selling and what niche you want to operate in. There are several ways you can make money from online auctions: you could sell your own product or sell products from others. The core essence of auctions is to find items at a cheap price to sell them at a higher price.

I will be showing you how you can make money selling items

on online auction sites, where you can buy items for cheap, the kind of items that are hot in demand, and how best to promote your commodities to make a profit.

How to Make Money from Online Auctions

The first thing to know is where to find items to sell. If you are going to be selling your own product, that's fine. If you are looking to source products, buy from suppliers, and promote yourself on the auction site, there are different strategies that can be used.

Finding Products: Because the main goal with an online auction is to sell for profit, you will need to find the right product that sells a lot at the right price. One great place to find products is **www.alibaba.com**. This is the biggest market of online retail goods' suppliers in the world. They are based in China and have over 130,000,000 different items on sale on the platform. You can find suppliers looking to sell unique products at rock bottom prices and still ship to any country across the world.

With suppliers on alibaba.com, you can comfortably set up your own store on any of the online auction sites.

There are other places you can find cheap items that you can put up. Look around you, there are garage sales going on, there is your immediate network, and there might even be friends trying to flip an item for quick cash. You can purchase items from any of these places and post on your store. People have made a killing by doing this.

Choose Your Platform: You have a range of auction websites to set up your business. EBay and uBid are the most popular, with eBay being the largest and having the most traffic. While I advise that you setup your store on eBay, also explore the other platforms and create a presence there. The important thing is that you are showing your merchandise to a larger audience. Setting up on eBay is free as it is with all the others, the only thing you have to pay attention to is using SEO and targeted advertising to promote your goods.

Promote Your Merchandise: The first thing to consider when promoting your goods is taking the right photograph. The products with crisp, clear images attract buyers the most. The buyer can get a clear physical description of what he or she is purchasing from the image. You also have to give an accurate description of the product so the buyer has an accurate expectation of the product. Most buyers trust sellers who are able to show what their product is about through a concise and clear description.

One other way you can further promote your goods is through advertising. You can pay for advertising your store.

You can leverage social media to further promote your goods.

Manage Customers: When your marketing efforts start to pay off, you will definitely become overwhelmed by the number of messages you receive. You will do right to utilize tools like VENDIO to help you manage all your clients' communications. You can use any of the major payment processing merchants such as PayPal to receive payments. Ensure that you set up shipping and delivery. If the cost is to be taken care of by the buyer, it should be clearly stated on the description of the item.

Other customer management setups include inventory, item tracking, automated check-out, etc.

Now that you have your store setup, you are ready to provide a great customer experience. Show respect to your customers and treat them the way you would want to be treated when you visit a store. The fact that you run a virtual auction does not give you the right to lose your manners. Customers will always return to where they were treated well.

Expand your market. Aside from alibaba.com there are other websites that have suppliers willing to sell to you at a bargain. According to history, the best-selling products have been electronics, video games and household goods. These products always have customers looking for a bargain. This business is usually filled with excitement and fun so have some fun while making money.

Final note: Do your research and stick with products that are in demand. The aim of the business is to make money and not to become a warehouse. The more deals you are able to close, the more profit you will earn.

CHAPTER 34 - PROGRAMMING

Programming is the act of creating a set of instructions that tell a computer how to perform certain tasks. This is a specialized skill and you would need to acquire training in order to use it to earn money online.

The world of computing as we know it is built on codes. Every graphic model or movie reel, web page, or application has long lines of written code behind it.

The world of programming is vast and its application spans different industries. This is what makes programming a viable venture to undertake. There are opportunities everywhere for a programmer. The job scope varies depending on what the customer wants to achieve. A programmer can be hired to write new codes from scratch or to clean up old code.

This is not to say that you must become a geek (even though I think geeks are great) but you must have an affinity for computers and must be smart, and I mean really smart. You must also be ready to work for long stretches at a time.

How Much Money?

There is no fixed amount that a freelance programmer can earn. But one thing is for sure; programmers are at the very top of the food chain. Programmers are one of the highest paid IT personnel. In my opinion, they should be. They make everything happen. In your exploits as a programmer, you would come to understand why they are paid so much.

Have you seen a programmer's computer screen when they are writing code? It stumps me how they are able to decipher information from the bulk of gibberish that's on their screen.

I tip my hat to them!

There are several factors that can also influence how much you can earn as a freelance programmer. The task at hand, your client's budget, and your bargaining power are a few indicators that determine your rates.

Freelance programmers at the basic level attract fees of up to $120 per hour. This seems fair in my opinion. You could earn more as your skill set improves and when you become a master of the craft.

Getting Started

There are skills you must possess before you can venture into programming. I am going to break it down a little here. Most programmers are identified by the kind of software they use in achieving their work. Not all software accomplish the same thing and even when they do, most times they are presented in different formats.

A good freelance programmer is someone who must have had experience in two or more programming languages. The various languages available to program are listed below:

1.	SQL

2.	JAVA

3.	C++

4.	Python

5.	RUBY

These are just a few of the common languages in use today. Knowledge of any of these languages is your first step to becoming a freelance programmer.

How to Become a Successful Programmer

There are few tips on how you can acquire the right skill, ways to promote your skills and places to find jobs.

Skills Acquisition

There are lots of ways you can acquire programming skills. The Internet is one good place to start. There is a large repository of information on Google. A quick search will present you with a wide variety of options on where to get free or paid training. The good thing about this is that all of your training, resources and tasks can be completed from the comfort of your own home. I have listed a few platforms that offer free training. I have found these websites to be very insightful and good enough to acquire the right knowledge. These platforms offer industry standard trainings.

W3schools.com: One of the most popular online platforms for free training on web design and web development is w3schools.com. It offers full curriculum training on JAVA and a comprehensive program that caters to web design, web development and web programming. And everything is free! You have the opportunity to learn web programming using Java, ASP.net and PHP. W3schools.com is one of the oldest platforms that offers free training for programming and is also currently the largest one.

Code Academy: This platform offers you a set of instructor led videos to learn from. The courses are structured in the form of a walk through interactive example method. Each example will show you how to develop skills in various programming languages, and from the examples you will gain knowledge and practice. The programs span languages such as

JAVA, RUBY, ASP.net and PHP. This platform is really great because it offers full courses on various programming languages, and all in example mode to aid quick assimilation of the process since you get to see the teaching applied in real time.

Khan Academy: Khan Academy is a non-profit online learning platform. It was founded by Salman Khan in 2006. It offers video courses on a variety of subjects including math and science. They have a rich curriculum that caters to programming languages like JAVA, ASP.net, PHP and C++.

Udemy: Udemy is one of the largest online learning marketplaces. It attracts instructors from over 112 countries and has had over 90 million people enroll for courses on their platform. They have courses on almost any language you desire and a vast array of instructors. The courses are video and instructor-led. Courses on Udemy are not free and they would set you back by about $250, depending on the pedigree of the instructor and the volume of coursework.

Skills Promotion

The first rule of thumb I want to share with you is that you should learn to set your expectations correctly.

You will need to earn the trust of your clients by delivering on time and within the scope of work that you promised. It is important that you only make promises that you know you can keep. When you do not have the required skills to perform a task, it is more honorable to decline the offer if you can't find someone better at it to help you, than to make promises that become difficult to fulfill.

There are a few ways you can promote your skills.

Join a Network: There are lots of networks on social media that cater solely to programmers. You can research these networks on Facebook and Reddit. Forums are a good place to stay informed about the latest news. You can make posts answering other people's questions or sharing information about what you have learned. Try to be active on all of your networks. Being active can get you the right visibility but be careful with what you post. Make sure your posts are error free and reflect your skill. You can call on others to assist with a project whenever you are overwhelmed or need insight. Referrals are easily gotten from these platforms.

Create your Website: You can design it yourself or have someone do it for you because a website is a great place to market your skills. You can direct prospective clients to your website so they can see what you have done in the past. If your skill is aligned with web programming, your website becomes a testing ground for new designs and ideas. This is how you display your creativity for the world to see. It should also serve as a gallery to display your works.

Where to Find Jobs

There are lots of people looking to hire programmers to perform simple to complex tasks on job boards, freelance platforms and social media sites. The key differentiating factor here is a good portfolio. Prospective clients would always want to evaluate your skill before committing to hiring you, so it is important that you create a good portfolio even if they are not for paying customers. This will help you in attracting clients and possibly getting you your first job.

Other Ways to Monetize Your Skill

You can further monetize your skills using other methods.

Another way you can still make money as a programmer is to offer customization services. You can create custom templates that perform specific tasks and sell them for a small fee, or you can offer up customization services for existing templates.

Your knowledge is vital. Alhough you might have gained knowledge for free, you can teach and get paid. There some busy people who just want someone to personally put them through easy tasks, and that's where you come in. Your activities on various networks can help get you get this sort of job..

Sharpen up Your Skills

Learning is continuous. You should never stop finding out what's new; always look for the latest trends and ways to perform tasks better. By now you have probably started making money so a little investment in refresher courses hosted by high level professionals in the industry will not hurt your pocket. Not only will they provide you with forums to network on, but they will expose you to people you can learn from and share knowledge with. Make good use of your spare time to continue to upgrade your skills.

Conclusion

I've outlined a number of methods on how to develop your skill, promote yourself and how to find jobs. This is a great way for you to make money but it will require you to put in lots of effort initially. Create your unique signature and stick with it so that you are able to establish a brand.

Work and income can be very sporadic so there is a need for good money management skills. Use the tips provided to improve your income, and search for new ways to master your craft and you will see that effort reflect in your earnings.

CHAPTER 35 - MOBILE APP DEVELOPMENT

Mobile application development is a subset of programming. We have discussed a great deal already on programming in a previous section; you can check that out for tips and tricks.

Mobile application development is the use of programming software to program an application to perform a specific task on a mobile platform.

They are basically two platforms that mobile apps are designed for, the iOS and Android. There are several tools to use in creating and developing your mobile app; the choice of what tool to use is solely at your discretion but it is important to note that not all of them are equal.

The most important components of mobile application architecture are mobile platforms, tools and frameworks, and application technology.

I will show you the best tools to use in creating and developing your mobile app. I will also walk you through the maze of what you need to set up and how you can market your skill. Training is available online if you have no prior knowledge.

How Much Money Can You Make as a Freelance Programmer?

There is no fixed pay structure for a mobile app developer but they are one of the highest paid in the field of information technology. A mobile application developer can earn huge sums, the job is very lucrative, and the services are high in demand.

The possibility for earning is quite expansive as the developer can earn from offering his or her services to a client. If an app begins to sell really well, income can be generated from adverts and sales.

Getting Started

The world is evolving at a very fast pace. There is a mobile app for almost anything now. Think about it though, there is a catch here. If mobile apps have become so popular, then how is there profitability in creating and developing an app?

Creating a mobile app is one way to generate a guaranteed steady income for life as long as your app stays relevant. A good mobile app developer is someone who must have had experience in two or more programming languages.

Idea

In the steps to creating a mobile app, the first one is to come up with an idea. Think carefully, look around you, there is a need to fulfill; there is a small task to automate. Research has shown that the most successful mobile apps are actually designed to solve small issues.

You could develop a game. Mobile games are great and they sell well. Or you could create an image editing app or a desktop processing app. Whatever idea you have, research it well, there must be an app already existing for it. Look at how you can better improve the existing app and then go ahead and make it. Do not relent in promoting your app and let the main selling point be the great user experience you have been able to create.

Your reach does not stop at just creating the next most popular app in world, but it can be extended to that local business that wants to reach mobile customers. More people now access web based platforms from mobile devices than they do from laptops or PC. The market for ideas in mobile app development is huge. When you become established you will realize that most of your clientele will be those who are looking to migrate to mobile or those looking to enhance their mobile applications. Your skill set should fit right in.

Choose Your Platform

There are numerous platforms for creating and developing mobile apps but like I had said earlier, they all are not equal. Some are good, others fair, some better, but there are those that are almost perfect for achieving a beautifully, fully functional mobile app.

For the purpose of knowledge, there are three fundamental mobile app architectures:

1.   **Native:** Native code architecture allows only one platform for the operation of the application. The application is stored on the device once downloaded, and it runs on the specific platform it was created for.

2.   **Cross-platform:** Cross-platform apps can run on multiple mobile platforms. These apps reside on the device and can be downloaded from any app store.

3.   **Mobile web apps:** Mobile web apps are designed to run over the Internet from a central server, and can be accessed from any device with a compatible browser.

Each approach has its own advantages and drawbacks and this is due to the differences in technology. The key is to understand the app requirements and deploy the right technology.

My personal choices of architecture are the cross-platform and the mobile web app. This is because these are the most scalable and flexible platforms. During the course of your work, you will come across situations that will cause you to use either platform and in some rare cases, you may have to use both of them.

PhoneGap is one of the best Cross-platform frameworks for mobile app development. The best one for creating mobile web apps is *Sencha*.

Where to Acquire Skills

There are lots of ways you can acquire the right skills. There is a large repository of information on Google and a quick search will present you with a wide variety of options on where to get free or paid training. The good thing about this is that all of your training, resources, and tasks can be completed from the comfort of your own home. I have listed a few platforms that offer training that I have found to be very insightful and good enough for you to acquire the right knowledge. These are the platforms that offer industry standard training:

Udacity.com: Udacity is the free online computer science class offered by Stanford University. It has got over 1.6 million users and is one of the largest and most popular open online courses. It was launched in 2012 and provides courses in the form of quizzes and short videos to keep the user engaged in the learning process. They offer free and paid access for courses on Android and iOS mobile application development.

Lynda: Lynda has existed since 1995, and since that time they have been offering video tutorials in different disciplines. Their mobile application program is broken into skill levels: beginner, intermediate and advanced. The courses are by industry experts and can be accessed in various languages.

CHAPTER 36 - SEO – SEARCH ENGINE OPTIMIZATION

SEO – Search Engine Optimization: This is a combination of actions that a professional undertakes to optimize for search engine websites and blogs.

Google is the most important and largest web search engines out there. It is here where websites compete for visibility. The better the strategy you apply for your website, the better visibility your platform will receive. With SEO, you are dealing with keywords, tags and meta tags.

An SEO freelancer is one of the most sought-after professionals in the industry. Every good businessman wants to be seen. Marketability in and of itself is highly dependent on being visible. The job of making a website, blog, or YouTube channel visible falls on the shoulders of the SEO professional. It doesn't stop there though. Even mobile app developers need SEO specialists. The impact on the industry cannot be overstated.

Your specific skill makes you in demand to both IT professionals and businesses alike.

How do You Make Money?

The job of an SEO professional is not a metered job. Your pay most times doesn't exist on a pay scale, but you can still make lots of money. There is a huge demand for these professionals who know their stuff and can make a good living for themselves.

There are some authorities in the field that are constantly running quick self-improvement courses on SEO. Take advantage of these opportunities to further develop your skills and also use them as platforms for making useful connections.

Getting Started

Below are some of the tasks that this role will require you to do.

Keyword Research: This is the first thing to know. Keywords are instrumental to unlocking the potential of SEO. If applied properly, they could help you hit your client's objective on the first try.

You need to understand how to research keywords. Depending on the niche, you have to look for the most called upon word. It's easy; avoid common words in the industry and look for words (seed words) that relate in some way to the popular words in that industry. Look out for the best combination of your keywords to achieve attainable and sufficient traffic.

There are tools that are also on the Internet that can help you find the right keywords for your site. It is important that you grow your skills and knowledge when developing keywords. Examples of tools that can be helpful in this regard include: Google Keyword Planner, Bing Keyword Research and Wordtracker Keyword Suggestion Tool.

On-Site Analysis Optimization: When implementing SEO, there are some key things to consider. SEO implementation is not a one size fits all kind of program. It is a combination of many things. You may have been able to find the right keywords but without proper optimization, your work is done in vain.

Tools like SEO Workers Site Analysis provide checklists of what you need to do in order to achieve a great SEO program.

The best way to start becoming a great SEO specialist is to have experience with whatever you hope to implement for a client. What better way to do that than to implement the same strategy on your website. You must have tested the strategies on your own platform first and monitored their effectiveness and progress. Using a checklist will help with this greatly.

Infuse keywords into metadata. Just don't overuse it.

Link Building: Links represent the off-site SEO implementation. The fact is that you would want to have people linking and referencing you client's website. More links inevitably lead to better traffic. But not to worry, there are ways to ensure that this will happen for your site. One of the best methods of achieving this is by guest posting and dropping links on social websites like Quora, Reddit and Mashable. Doing this gives your website more credibility.

The search engine bots are a lot smarter today, only content that offers user value are propelled to the first page. So make sure that as you build your backlinks, they are followed up by great content.

There are a couple of tools that will also help you achieve your desired results in SEO rankings. Haro is one such tool. While you're at it, do not forget to also check out WordPress SEO tools for further assistance on backlink building. Allpro is also a good one to look at as well.

Finding Work

There are a lot of places where you can find work as an SEO specialist.

Freelance Platforms: The easiest places are still the major freelance platforms. There are businesses that use Upwork and Fiverr who are looking for SEO specialists to undertake their web promotion. You just have to create a great profile and if you are asked for previous experience, you can have them check yours out. You don't have to wait until you have worked with a client before you can claim experience. Utilize your website as a practice ground, since this further reinforces what I said earlier in this guide. Be certain that you will have to practice a great deal. Ensure to monitor results and keep track of your progress.

Advertise: You could also place targeted ads on Google or Facebook that advertise your skills. This is also a test of your skill. The better you are able to gain visibility for your website, the easier it will be to achieve the same for a client. Invest in PPC ads for better SEO, as well as other forms of targeted ads. Please ensure you apply good money management practices; you don't want to start spending so much when you haven't made any money.

Social Networks: You can leverage your social networks to get connections that can help get more business. Offer a free service to a nonprofit institution; it's a great way of gaining visibility.

On a final note, you will need to practice a lot. Research tools on the Internet, some may require you pay a fee, but that's fine if the resource is worth it. Always keep learning.

CHAPTER 37 - ONLINE SURVEY

An online survey from the early days of the Internet has been one of the best and easiest ways to make money online. There are a lot of paid surveys that are currently running online for you to make consistent income. Once you get the hang of this, you can either hire others to do surveys for you, or you can create your own survey website. One of these two steps will ultimately turn the income into passive income.

Paid online surveys are surveys conducted by companies or organizations seeking market data that help them to tailor their products and services to better fit the market. These surveys are usually conducted by survey panels on behalf of the businesses.

Survey questions usually range from 10 to 100. This is largely dependent on the motive for the survey and how much the panel is offering. You can get paid between $0.50 to as high as $5 per survey. It may seem like a little but when aggregated across various panels, you can find yourself finishing as many as 10 to 50 surveys per week by just taking 10 minutes of your time. Do the math!

Some surveys will only require a short time and will still pay a premium. I will show you the best surveys and how to maximize your earnings.

Getting Started

To get started, you will need to have a computer or tablet and the Internet. You have to find a reliable survey panel to register on in order to start getting surveys.

These are some of my personal picks:

1.   Mysurveys

2.   Inboxdollars

3.   Swagbucks

4.   Opinion Outpost

Once you have registered and completed your profile, the survey panel will send you surveys that match your profile. In the email you receive, details of the survey will be provided. These details will include things like the time taken, how much you will get paid, and where to fill out the survey.

Once you have taken quite a number of surveys, and have been able to earn some substantial money, you can apply to withdraw it and your money will be credited to your account. The payment processor usually used is PayPal. Companies seeking your opinion make payments to the survey panels that then pay you for sharing.

Below are some things to watch out for.

Be mindful of survey panels asking you to make payment during registration as they may be a scam. To belong to a panel is free. Most panels are looking for members and they do not charge registration fees.

Just as there are many reputable panels, there are just as many scam panels. These panels will only succeed at wasting your time and in severe cases, steal your money or identity.

To find reliable survey panels, I would suggest you research platforms that conduct a review of survey panels. I have listed my personal best panels above, you should check those out. I can vouch for their reliability. But do not limit yourself to just those ones and look around on the Internet. You will find many more that are reliable and profitable.

There are a few other things to look out for to determine if a survey panel is legitimate or a scam.

1.   Avoid survey panels that ask for membership fees.

2.   Do the same with panels that promise a fixed income.

3.   Survey platforms with unrealistic high commissions.

4.   If there is no explicit communication on compensation.

5.   If the panel does not have a privacy policy, then don't join it.

Be mindful that not every panel shown on Google is legit. Conduct your due diligence by properly researching survey panels and also read reviews of their offers, paying particular attention to their compensation plans, how frequently they send out surveys, and what they require during registration.

Note that not all surveys pay in cash. Some surveys pay in gift cards, coupons or free access to paid services. So be clear on the compensation before completing the survey.

Maximize Your Earnings

There are a couple of tricks you can use with paid online surveys. Although they may not make you rich, they have the ability to provide passive income to take care of some bills.

The basic trick here is to get push notifications for your email. Because the communication between you and the survey panel is via email, you have to know when surveys are sent to you and you must answer them promptly. This is because most surveys operate on a first-come first-serve basis. You need to be in the loop at all times to be able to take full advantage of the benefits that a survey has to offer.

Ensure that your profile is always up to date. This is what the panels look at before sending you a survey. Tailor your profile to fit high paying niches. Always take the survey with the highest commission first before taking any other one.

Register on as many survey platforms as possible. Like I have said before, the value is in the numbers. A single survey may not seem like great value, but when aggregated across all other platforms, the amount starts to look really good. Surveys will definitely not make you rich but they will provide enough money to pay some bills or other expenses.

CHAPTER 38 - ONLINE CONSULTANCY

Online consultancy is one online business that can be started up with no capital whatsoever. The only requirement to start this sort of business that can guarantee you financial freedom is your knowledge. What specific knowledge do you have? Your knowledge is being sorted out online. In this guide, I will show just how easy it is to set up an online consultancy business with just a laptop, phone and the Internet.

Most people just like you are not aware of a number of small businesses that need their specific knowledge to thrive. You do not require any form of capital or even an office space to set up your online consultancy business. The skills you need are very good networking skills, marketing skills, good communication skills and the knowledge you are bringing to bear on the businesses you will be consulting.

Getting Started

In this business of online consulting, knowledge is your currency. Consultants are in very high demand as they provide insights to business challenges and help forge an actionable plan for growth for the target business. If you know your stuff, the number of businesses you will be consulting for will grow in no time as the news of your expertise spreads.

There are a few tips I am going to share with you to help you get a head start in this business.

The Right Mindset: This business is not for the faint at heart, however. Have you ever tried selling something intangible? That's the way it is with selling consultancy. You need to be able to convince the client that you have everything it takes to provide advice and offer solutions to growing their business. It's going to be hard, but with the right mindset, the winning mindset, you will get your first client and when you do, deliver on all your key objectives. This will bolster your reputation and improve your confidence to take on bigger clients.

Focus your efforts: Businesses are not the only ones that require the services of a consultant. Consultancy cuts across all major disciplines. There are consultants in fashion, security, IT, food, safety, health care, nutrition, engineering, HR, accounting and education.

Whatever discipline you fall under, you can set up a consultancy for that niche, but be sure to obtain all the necessary permits, including tax and business licenses.

Have a Structured Business Plan: This is very important if you want to succeed. A business plan is very important for any business that is starting out as it serves as a roadmap for the business. Your business plan should contain a financial plan, a marketing strategy and a management plan. The business plan should be structured and organized in a manner that shows the idea and business direction of your consultancy setup.

Print Stationery: This is maybe the only major expense you will incur. You'll need to print out business cards, letterheads and call cards. This gives your business a measure of branding. Most people like structure and will naturally do business with you if they sense there is some form of structure. Do not hesitate to pass your business card around anytime you are in contact with anyone who may need your services.

Ensure that the design of your card is visually appealing and attractive.

Connect and Build Relationships: This is the most effective way to grow your business and find clients. Your skill alone can't get you those jobs, you will need to go out and connect daily with people who need your service. Attend conferences, meetings and programs. Make use of social media to further promote your business. The more visible you are, the more likely it is that you are going to land a client. You should always give premium service to those who give your business a chance. Build relationships with them and encourage them to share the good word on your behalf.

Work for Free: Some free work won't hurt your business. It is even a good way to advertise your skill. This is also a way to gain experience since when you are starting out, most businesses would want to be convinced that you have what it takes to deliver. One of the easiest ways to convince them of this is by showing previous work.

You can provide this free work for your friends, family or even a non-profit business who you think may require your service.

Partner with Other Businesses and Consultant Groups: You would have to learn from those who have gone before you. Join a network of consultants within your niche. This does not limit your opportunity to get work, but rather it provides you with a platform to grow your business through collaboration. You will learn a lot from these groups. It will help with referrals, it can also serve as a validation point so that you can say, "I am a member of XYZ consultants action group, a group setup to promote safe and efficient engineering" if you are indeed in the engineering group. If you have these sorts of statements in your bio, it confers on you a seemliness of value and authority. That's not to say you are not valuable or you are not an authority, but this is to just show you how to appeal to the sense of value of the business you are looking to consult.

Promote Your Business

There are many ways you can promote your business. But the best way is for you to make good use of your network. It is important that you develop relationships and harness them for the growth of your business.

You can also promote your business on freelance websites. There are a lot of businesses looking to engage consultants for work. Promotions on these platforms are free and you can get a lead from there. I also encourage you to set up a website and promote it across your social media profiles. Share insightful posts relating to the services you offer and ask others to do same.

You can start a free series on your Facebook or Twitter. You should make posts that can help businesses in your niche on a regular basis and in no time, you will start getting sales.

Consultancy is not a piece of cake, it is a serious business. Taking shape may be a little slow at first, but just keep at it. Pursue consistency and whenever you have the opportunity to work, "wow" the client and build a relationship to let that work for you. Do not neglect networks of similar professionals. Attend conferences, meetings and lunches where you will have the opportunity to network. Try to be visible on all fronts and at all times strive to deliver on your objectives.

CHAPTER 39 - WEBSITE FLIPPING

Website flipping is similar to domain flipping, but what is being flipped is a website instead. There are a few things that differentiate domain flipping from website flipping, and that is with domain flipping there is no need to enhance the domain. Unlike website flipping, you would need to make a significant investment in time and creative resources to turn a website into a high-value asset.

The business of website flipping is a lucrative one no doubt, but you will need keen insight and proper research to make it big in this field. There are those who have done it and have been very successful at it. Some websites have been flipped and sold for as much as 4,000% more than the original amount.

To start trading in websites, you must think "value." That's the only way to get the maximum return on your investment. If you have gone through SEO consultancy in the web design section, you would understand what value is to a website. I will advise you check it out but just so you have an idea, the important attributes of a high-value website is its SEO and backlinks.

What is its SEO program like? How many reputable backlinks redirect to it. These factors determine the value of a website.

Getting Started

When starting out in website flipping, I advise you start small. Make your investment in bits and learn as you go along. There is no need to hurry, there are over 300,000 websites registered daily so there are always good bargains to pick from.

This is the catch; people set up websites for various reasons, if that purpose is not achieved, they tend to abandon the project. You can get access to their website if they abandon it and it expires, or you can purchase it from them for a small fee. You need to be very business savvy and have a keen eye to make money here. You also have to be ready to research extensively to determine the value of a prospect and also to develop the ones in your portfolio so that they attract good value.

These websites can be bought by you for peanuts and then sold for hundreds if not thousands of dollars. Because new businesses are always looking for popular websites and domains, you can cash in on this and make some good money for yourself. Your responsibility is to find good websites, make them yours for peanuts, develop them extensively, and then sell to eager buyers.

With website flipping, you have to dedicate yourself to understanding the market; the niche that is fast selling, how to generate traffic, the best SEO technique to use, how to implement backlinks, and finally the design.

You may be tempted to want to build a website from scratch but I would advise against that for obvious reasons. It is my opinion that you want to develop a business model that has a good turnover rate, right? If this is the case, and it should be, the amount of time and resources it will take to build a site from scratch and develop it to the point where it can command a fair value is quite long. You could be at it for a year or more.

So what is the best approach? I will show you how you can purchase websites with some value for cheap, how to develop them, and then how to sell them for a high return.

Finding the Right Website

Deciding on the right website to purchase for flipping is essential to your success in this business.

Pick a Niche: The niche you decide on is also an important factor to consider. The highest grossing niches are health and fitness, sports and lifestyle. This is not to say that the other niches aren't profitable, but these are the ones that have brought good returns on investment in the shortest possible time.

Research: This is something you should be doing throughout your sojourn in this business. It may get easier over time but it does not stop, so get used to it. There are a few things you must keep in mind when researching websites. Your research will always take two forms. First, you have to find out the best website that is cheap, and secondly, you need to learn how to develop the website to the point where it can give you more value.

The best place to look when researching websites is on the Internet. Search Google for high traffic niches and go far into the 10th to 20th page to look in for potential prospects. If you find something you like, check the contact us page and contact the owner.

Note: there are penalized websites that cost next to nothing that you can also make an investment into and revamp for a good sale. I will discuss that later.

Avoid Scams: There are lots of scams on the Internet. If you sense anything shady about the website or its promoter, I will advise that you back out of the deal.

Marketing Your Website

After developing your new website, you will need to find a way to sell it for profit. There are several online platforms that cater to these sorts of things. Let us take a look at some of them. You can also find great bargains for websites on these platforms. Just look out and take the points we have listed above into consideration.

Below are some of the best places to start your website flipping venture.

1.   **Flippa Marketplace:** Flippa is the best marketplace for trading websites and apps. It is one of the most popular platforms in the website auction space.

Most people come here to spend money. About 40% of visitors end up making trades. Your websites will have the best visibility here.

2.   **Sedo Website Marketplace:** Sedo is one of the leading website trading marketplaces available. Sedo has over 2 million member accounts from around the world, all trading in websites and domain names. There is a huge market for your website here.

Sedo connects buyers with sellers to create an easy and smooth transaction experience. With over 18 million websites on sale, Sedo is the largest marketplace for websites.

3.   **Website Broker:** Website Broker is a marketplace primarily designed to trade websites. In spite of this, domains are also traded on the platform. This is a great place to advertise your website. Sometimes you can cash in on a good bargain here. People are constantly advertising their websites on this platform.

4.   **EBay:** eBay is one of the best places to sell websites online. You can find cheap websites here too. People are always looking to flip their websites and on a good day, you can strike a bargain. Just make sure that you do your homework before consenting to a transaction.

5.   **Brand Bucket:** The brand bucket is one of the very popular platforms for website flipping. They only trade in quality, unique and high-valued websites. Most websites on Brand Bucket attract prices in the thousands of dollars. This is one of the best platforms to trade websites. The opportunity for profits here is huge.

Key Points

Trading websites can be a little risky but it is highly profitable. It requires patience and tack to make it big here. Conduct your due diligence and make sure you have a written down objectives for any web asset you acquire. This will help you chart a roadmap on how to go about your investment.

To successfully trade in websites profitably, you will need to make some major investments. But not to worry, it will pay off if you apply the strategies I have taught here. The profit margins in website flipping are usually quite high, so what you require to at least break even is just one sale.

It is important to practice money management skills as well. Take it slow, start small. Once you have made a few trades and have started to gain practical experience, you can then move on to bigger turf.

CHAPTER 40 - ONLINE SUBSCRIPTION SERVICE

Subscription services have been around for a while. They were used primarily by newspapers and magazines, and have only just migrated online in recent times. Today a variety of stuff is delivered on a periodic basis to customers all across America, and most of these transactions originate and are fulfilled online.

An online subscription service is one of those services that still find a market in almost every home, and the potential is still growing. Different categories and sizes of items are being delivered to homes in America every day and more people are signing up to subscription services that cater to their needs.

Today, items such as hampers filled with groceries are shipped daily to clients who have subscribed to the service. Cigarettes, snacks and even drinks are now common items delivered to subscribers. So how can you take advantage of this opportunity? Let me show you.

Originally, an online subscription service was a marketing strategy adopted by large manufacturers and wholesalers to further expand their market share and guarantee sales every month, but it has now been adopted by small businesses serving various niches that were not covered by mainstream subscription services.

The beauty of an online subscription service is the fact that it requires very little capital to setup and offers variety. You are open to a large number of vendors offering a wide variety of products to choose from; all you have to do is to create the right sales platform and market it across your entire network.

Online subscription services as a marketing strategy is constantly evolving and reaffirming its stand. It's a good investment with great prospects, although like all businesses, there are few challenges that this guide will address.

Getting Started

There are a number of things to consider before engaging in this service. You have to understand that although it is an online service, you will need to meet offline with vendors and wholesalers. You may require extra space, but you can take advantage of drop shipping services to reduce your overhead. There is no heavy startup cost. Subscribers have paid up front for the service, so if the process is handled properly by you, it can be quite seamless. You just have to follow through on the points I will enumerate below and then you will be ready to start up.

Things to Consider:

Find Your Niche: Is it a mono product service? Are you only providing one product for your clients? Or is it a multi product service?.

It is important you carry out extensive market research, take note of competition, look into what they are doing, what products they're offering, value added services, etc. This will help give you a wholesome understanding of the business and help you fashion a winning strategy.

It is also important that you focus on a niche that you know and understand. Do not look at your service as a seller but more as a consumer. Having some sort of understanding of the market is very important to help you match competition, and to also deliver effective and efficient service.

Find Vendors/Wholesalers: Depending on the kind of service you hope to offer, you have to look for vendors in the industry to get supplies for you. Vendors are key partners in this business. Your supplier's product quality is very crucial to your success.

First, you want to check your area to find businesses. Once you have covered your immediate locality, you can proceed online to search for credible wholesalers.

Note: I am taking it from the standpoint of a multi-product strategy and with particular emphasis on essentials like grocery boxes to be delivered monthly, lunch packs, supplies, and general home essentials. This is not all that is covered by online subscriptions, as you can also offer various services. A monthly tax return done remotely for small businesses falls under online subscriptions as long as the clients are willing to pay regularly, or buy a period plan in exchange for your services.

Choose Your Product – Add Value: With a lot of competition in the market, it is only logical that you look for ways to better the offers given by competitors. Conduct research extensively and come up with ways you can add value to the product you offer. Nothing is vague or of no importance. A little thank you note of appreciation as you drop off the item can go a long way in retaining customers and converting new ones. You don't have to spend money, consider your business and look at how you can better offer that service. That's adding value.

We can also look at another illustration of what someone in fashion can do to add value. (Did I tell you that fashion is one of the hottest niches? Well, it is and services in fashion tailored to specific individuals are also a great idea.)

So, you have finally decided on promoting a business involved in the fashion industry. They operate a dry-cleaning service that caters only to suits; one of the ways you can add value is to provide scale charts on how to decide on the right kind of suit for your body structure, a guide on the choice of material, or instructions on how to pair suit accessories.

This may seem little, but it is of great importance. Just imagine the number of people whose buying decision would be based just on the information you provide. At all times, there is a value added service that you can provide. Also look out for ways to better the experience of your clients.

Whatever value added service you decide to offer, try all you can to make sure that the product is of great quality. This is the basic value experience you need to have for all your customers.

Design a Sales Platform: This is where all your marketing efforts come to. It is on this platform that customers get to see the products you have on offer. This is where you receive your requests, make sales and manage orders. Depending on your scale and financial prowess, there are a lot of options to choose from. You can start small and move on to bigger platforms from there.

The more standard method is to take advantage of the solutions offered by the likes of Shopify. All you require to have your own online store up and running is to sign up on Shopify and they will do the rest. They will help you build and launch your own website from A-Z with no technical hassles.

Author's Note

Thank you again for purchasing this book!

I hope this book was able to help you learn more about the various passive income and online business ideas that are out there.

The next step is to share with others what you have learned here.

Finally, if you enjoyed this book then I'd like to ask you for a favor. Would you be kind enough to leave a review for this book on Amazon? It'd be greatly appreciated!

Thank you and good luck!

Preview of "Instagram Marketing" by David J Green

Instagram has undergone a complete metamorphosis, from an iOS app it was originally designed to become to a huge social media site with tons of benefits both for private individuals and businesses. Over the years, the platform has shown no sign of losing its growth, not with the backing of the mighty Facebook. That should reassure you that its growth in recent years is not a fluke, but will continue for years to come.

From that small beginning a couple of years ago, Instagram now has over 700 million active users and some 400 million daily active users from all walks of life according to some reports on social media sites and some research institutes. That's not all, the mobile industry is increasing at an alarming rate with more than 20 billion photos shared in 2014 and over 100 million users daily active on social media. What role did Instagram play in the sudden surge of using social media sites for businesses?

Instagram has grown to become a formidable social media site and a powerful marketing tool for business owners in different niches across the world. According to some data collected from different sources, people are gradually shifting from Facebook and Twitter to Instagram due to the tons of benefits that Instagram offers, especially for businesses, companies, and brands. This is responsible for the sudden surge in the number of daily active users on Instagram.

A recent study also revealed that Instagram performs 58 times better than Facebook and 120 times better than Twitter. These are awesome statistics that prove that Instagram has evolved from a pushover app to a powerful stakeholder in the social media circle. This made it take a spot among the best social media tools for business promotion and increased customer engagement and conversion. Consider these interesting Instagram marketing statistics that support the rapid growth of the social media site:

- Over 70% of brands have Instagram accounts.

- Over 90% of the top 100 brands in the world are active on Instagram.

- 96 % of US fashion brands have an Instagram presence.

- According to comScore in its 2014 Mobile Trends report, "And if you're looking to target millennials, the numbers are even better: With 42% penetration of millennial smartphone users, they spend more than an astounding 439 minutes per month on the platform [Instagram]."

Since the millennials form the larger chunk of the target audience for most businesses, their presence on Instagram is an indication of their acceptance of the site, and the potential benefits it offers.

These stats show the increasing impact of Instagram on people's social and business lives. The site has gradually grown from a kids' hangout to one of the biggest and most influential social media sites with the potential for helping your business grow and succeed.

The good news is that the popularity and increased user base of Instagram make it a viable business tool for online entrepreneurs, regardless of whatever their business may be. Many popular brands have leveraged the power of social media to grow their businesses into formidable businesses with a huge increase in popularity and huge turnover over the years.

Among the popular brands are Audi, National Geographic, Grand Central Station, Go Pro, Nike, and a host of others. These giants, in different business niches, have carved a niche for themselves on the platform as proof of the versatility of use and the powerful influence that Instagram can wield on a business.

However, using Instagram to boost your business requires you to take a crucial step: increase your Instagram follower base.

Increasing your Instagram followership is easier said than done if you are in the dark about the rules governing how you can effectively use the platform to take your business outreach to the next level.

As a newcomer to the game, you will have to face tons of obstacles, blatant misconceptions, baseless propaganda, and other negative ideas that may discourage you from taking advantage of Instagram to boost your business.

However, you can overcome any challenge you might face and increase your Instagram followership with the right tools and practical tips. These tips are discussed extensively in this book.

When you go through the book, you will learn some practical tips and salient points that will boost your morale and allay your fears. These are:

- Tips for growing your Instagram followership.

- The misconception about using Instagram for business.

- The challenges of using Instagram for business.

- How to solve your Instagram challenges.

- The benefits of using Instagram to grow your business.

- What you need to know about Instagram.

- How to create an effective Instagram marketing strategy.

- Top Instagram marketing strategies you should know.

- Top Instagram fails and how to avoid them.

It is my goal to teach you about the best social media practices so that you can explore the potentials of Instagram and maximize the benefits offered by the platform.

With this book, you can use these practical tips to easily grow your Instagram account and leverage that to get more referral traffic to your own website.

With that said, it is now time to delve deep into the book and fish out the hidden treasures contained within.

Chapter 1: Practical tips for growing your followership and increasing your fan base

You can't leverage the power of Instagram to boost your business if your followership is low. Come to think of it, you need people to patronize you and help your business grow. That implies that your business' success depends not on creating an Instagram account, but on the ability of the account to generate sufficient organic traffic through improved engagement and increased followership that can be directed to your website to boost your sales or patronage.

In line with this, there is a direct connection between your business and Instagram account: your fan base will directly determine how far your business can thrive amidst the stiff competition from your formidable competitors. If your fan base is too low, you shouldn't expect a miracle. It has nothing positive to offer your business and that can have an adverse effect on it. Their impact will depend on their numerical strength and that is a fact that you simply can't ignore.

Conversely, a massive fan base is an indication that you can get an impressive engagement and better conversion from your Instagram followers to your brand's website through awesome engagement.

This highlights the urgency and importance of having a huge followership that can greatly impact your business positively in all aspects. What practical steps can you take to achieve this?

There are tons of practical techniques that you can implement to increase the popularity and engagement of your Instagram account. These techniques will offer you the tools to gradually take your business, or brand image, to the Instagram community with a goal of expanding your reach to get more followers who have the potential for becoming your clients or customers.

A look at some of these effective methods will give you an idea of how you can leverage the power of Instagram to increase your followership to an enviable size with the potential for driving your business forward.

Within a couple of weeks after constant practice and consistency, you can grow your audience with these simple and effective tips:

Use Instagram hashtags effectively

Using hashtags is a common feature of some social media sites such as Instagram and Twitter. Hashtags are used for different functions on these sites such as making a topic trend and garnering more users to increase the engagement of a particular topic. Aside from using these hashtags to make some topics or posts go viral, you can also use hashtags to increase your followership if you understand how to use these effectively for the better performance for your posts.

Some of these rules involve being conversant with the latest hashtags, knowing what hashtags are appropriate for a particular situation, and which of the hashtags you can use effectively to have the desired impact on your account.

Let me explain some of these rules and how you can use them to achieve your goal.

- **Use special hashtags**

Although there are tons of hashtags on Instagram, they are not all used for the same purpose. Some are specifically created to help users gain more followers and have increased engagement. Some of these special hashtags are #l4l (Like for like), #followback, #FF (Follow Friday), #tagforlikes, and other hashtags with similar features. Using these hashtags on your images is tantamount to extending a direct invitation to other users on the platform to follow you. Many people will respond positively to the invitation and contribute to the growth of your account if your page has desirable content.

- **Be conversant with the best hashtags**

The Instagram community uses thousands of tags daily. This can range from business hashtags and celebrity hashtags, to economics and politics hashtags. Technically, you have tons of hashtags to choose from, depending on your business line. However, the question is which of these tags is the best one to use to ensure increased awareness for your brand? That requires that you need to be abreast of the new and the best hashtags, always. How can you do that? You have to look for them. Yes, literally comb the Internet and other social media resources to compile a comprehensive list of the best hashtags to choose from.

Knowing the best tag requires that you have a way of identifying the best tags based on some parameters that include their levels of engagement and their popularity among the Instagram community.

While that is practically impossible to manually go through all the tags in the world to check their engagement levels and their popularity among other users, rest assured that the Internet world does not leave the job to you alone. You have several digital tools at your disposal to help. One such tool is

Websta. This Instagram viewer will give you a comprehensive analysis and an exhaustive list of the best tags to choose from. Websta always compiles a list of the top 100 tags so that any interested person can view the list and have an idea of what the top tags are at that moment. You can avail yourself of this opportunity to reduce your stress and conserve your time if you decide to personally conduct research on the topic.

These are the best hashtags on Instagram at the writing of this book:

- #love (1.12 billion)

- #instagood (621.7 million)

- #photooftheday (436.7 million)

- #beautiful (404.8 million)

- #fashion (400.6 million)

- #tbt (379.1 million)

- #cute(376.3)

- #followme (347 million)

- #like4like (345.5 million)

- #follow (333 million)

Other hashtags that complete the first 20 best hashtags are:

- #me

- #selfie

- #summer

- #instadaily

- #friends

- #art

- #girl

- #nature

- #instalike

You can view the complete list of the top 100 Instagram hashtags on the Websta website whenever you want to find out what the best tags are. The first tag on this list has over a billion uses while the last can boast over 300 million uses. This shows the potentials hidden within these top tags. You can tap into the opportunity offered by these tags and increase your followership. Use the appropriate tag from the list with your photo and see a sharp increase in your brand awareness.

- **Take advantage of the autocomplete feature**

Instagram has an abundance of hidden gems that only experienced Instagram users can uncover. One such hidden gem is the autocomplete feature. The feature is the breeding ground for better hashtags with the potential to make your Instagram photo go viral. It has a similar functionality to Google's autocomplete feature that gives you numerous suggestions when using a search query to look for a product or information.

Just like its Google counterpart, the feature gives you a list of different alternatives to the hashtag you already have in mind when searching, so that you can use the better alternative with your photos and have more effective hashtags that can support your goal of increasing your fan base via your photos. From the list, you can choose the tag with the best user amount. Using the best hashtag increases your chances of getting the desired recognition by people online. Take a look at the list above again. The first 10 garnered over 3 billion uses. That offers you more value than perhaps the last 10 on the top 100 list. Imagine the potential increase in value that would occur just by using any one of them and what impact that will have on your brand.

- **Find the best hashtag in your niche**

A very important step towards driving traffic to your business Instagram account is having a good knowledge of the best hashtag in your business niche. It will be out of order if you don't know what works well in your business line. If you don't take the time to learn this, you are denying yourself the opportunity to have the best tool at your disposal. What's more is that you can also commit the unpardonable blunder of using the wrong hashtag if you don't know how to use tags for your images. For instance, what impact will using a politics-related hashtag have on your business when you are not promoting any political agenda? Do you think that using the hashtags that are ideal for vacation will have a favourable impact on your business?

These are different topics that require different hashtags to succeed. You need to use the appropriate hashtags to convey the corresponding message to your target audience and get them more involved in your campaign. When you know the best tags in your business line, you can work towards using them for personal causes so that you can have a shot at increasing your popularity on the social media platform. That is the way to grow, not the other way around. Otherwise, your best efforts may be insufficient to take your business beyond your warehouse or office.

Contrary to the general misconception about the difficulty of finding the most appropriate hashtags on Instagram, finding the best hashtags in your niche is relatively easy. The rule of thumb stipulates that you pay undivided attention to how other users in your target audience use some hashtags effectively. Take a cue from them and tweak the hashtags you have already known to help you succeed.

You only need a note-taking app where you can write down whatever tag you find useful, analyze the tag, and to see what other ways you can use the tags to suit your needs and increase your followership. One of the most effective apps for such purpose is the Simplenote app. This cross-platform app is ideal for taking notes whenever you find the right hashtag you want to jot down. You can also use the app on different platforms without restrictions or limitations.

Another valuable tool is the cheat sheet. This sheet can take the pressure off of going through a mammoth post daily in search of valuable tags from you. The clean sheet gives you a head start by offering you a comprehensive list of these hashtags and the best way to use them for your benefit. That way, you will spend a little less time on searching for the hashtags and direct your attention on how to best use the hashtags.

The Internet has tons of cheat sheets to choose from. They are well designed to simplify your search and give you the best assistance. Among these sheets, Tagstagram has proven itself to be the best and the most useful. It contains the best hashtags in an array of topics such as food, animals, politics, business, and the like. To further simplify your search, it also divides the hashtag into subdivisions for easy identification and proper use. For instance, the "Celebrities" section of Tagstagram contains different hashtags for celebrities such as Neymar, Rihana, as well as several others. You only need to choose the appropriate gender to find the hashtag for a particular celebrity.

The same principle can be adapted to your business. You can check the "Brand" or "Small Businesses" section for business-related hashtags that may address your particular need. You can unleash your power of imagination to make the tags useful for you. With repeated tweaking, you will get the best use out of these hashtags. If you have a clear idea of what you want, getting the most appropriate tag won't be difficult with these resources.

You can download the Tastagramapp on your mobile device to make it easy and convenient for you to access those tags, and constantly find better ways to use them effectively. On the other hand, if you can't download it for whatever reason, the platform has a responsive website that makes browsing easy for any user. That will make your search simple while you have access to tons of valuable information.

Some other tools you can use to find the best hashtags includes the TagsForLife website and Webstagram. The former tool gives you a long list of the best hashtags you can use for your images. After finding the best one for your niche, copy the tags and paste them in your photo. You are good to go. With the latter tool, you have direct access to the best hashtags you can use for making your posts more popular and gaining a larger audience.

In a nutshell, you can never run out of good tools that will simplify your search for what you need for improving your reach on Instagram.

- **Know the most appropriate tag for each day**

Building an impressive profile on Instagram is not possible within a short period of time. It is a long-term project with long-term benefits. You must regularly update your account with photos of your brand to keep people aware of the business. This fact raises a vital point: knowing the most appropriate tag for a particular day.

The hidden truth is that Instagram has different tags that are specifically designed for each day. This secret is known by a privileged few and is used to increase their fan base daily.

For instance, the hashtag for Monday is different from that of Tuesday and so on. Some days may have multiples of hashtags based on certain factors. Do you know the hashtags for each day? If you do, that's great. You must devise a practical way to leverage that knowledge to increase your fan base.

And if you don't, simple research will give you a list of the recognized hashtags for each day of the week. If you can follow the trend, your account will be boosted daily until you have a fan base that is large enough to impact your business positively.

Whether you come out with #fitnesssaturday, #motivationsunday, or #throwbackthursday, find the specific hashtag for a particular day and use it. You can reach out to a larger audience if you decide to participate in these day-specific hashtags.

- **Use relevant tags only**

The fact that you have thousands of Instagram hashtags doesn't give you the freedom to spam your post with hashtags. You can't incorporate any number of hashtags in your post just because you feel inclined to use the hashtags that way. Instagram has a limitation on the number of hashtags that can be used for a post. According to the social media site, you are limited to 30 hashtags per post. However, using all 30 in a single post is synonymous to spamming your picture. There is a stiff penalty for violators of this rule.

What do you do to protect yourself from getting Instagram's disapproval and punishment? Use the most relevant tags that will give you the best result. It is not really about the number of hashtags you can stuff in a post; it is about how well you can use them to maximize your chances of getting a better audience for your posts.

According to some social media experts, you can get the best results from a maximum of 5 tags. The only rule is to combine those tags well so that it can have a positive impact on your post, thereby leading to an overall improvement in your followership. If you find a working formula to combine the five tags effectively, it will guarantee you a better result than combining some tags randomly without a specific order or purpose for the combination.

Although there is no fixed rule that you can't exceed 5 hashtags, doing so should be with the goal of getting a better result rather than combining them "just because," or because you have seen some people with tons of tags attached to a post.

If you must exceed these 5 hashtags, a simple rule will give you the best result: don't use any tag in the picture caption so that your picture may look attractive and tidy. On the other hand, include the most appropriate tags in the first comment on the picture. That will give you the desired effect. Just know the rules and abide by them.

You must be conscious of the fact that you are a different entity, unlike the other guy whose posts you have seen with more than the suggested number of hashtags. You have no justifiable reason to copy his posting style. You don't have the same goal. You may even be in a completely different business terrain. Identify what will work for you, not what works for others. Identify the tags that will work well with you and combine them effectively. Monitor your pictures and see the impact of the tags you use on their popularity. That will give you a clue about the best tag for you. You can't achieve that by imitating someone's style without knowing the rationale behind that style.

If you use these tips as suggested, you will spare yourself the difficult task of having to dig through a heap of hashtags to find the best ones for you. With a little consistency, you will finally arrive at the best solution, the right formula for making the most effective use of Instagram hashtags to improve your account followership and fan base.

Let your account be easy to follow

People won't know about the existence of your account if your account is not conspicuous enough. You can only expect an appreciable growth in your followership if your account is easy to follow and encourages easy engagement. The more visible your account and photos are, the higher the number of people that will be aware of your business. That may translate to a literal increase in your popularity, and subsequently, your patronage. An Instagram account with a huge fan base is a gold mine that should be explored, rather than hidden.

However, some Instagram users have the unhealthy habit of making their accounts very difficult to follow. This may be through their strict settings that restrict access to their accounts or through a nonchalant attitude towards making their accounts visible to more people by sharing on other social media platforms such as Facebook. That is a destructive habit that you won't find amusing to imitate due to its potential negative and discouraging impact on your brand.

Your list of priorities should include making your profile very visible and easy to follow. That will make it easy for millions of future clients or customers to see your posts and engage with them. There are some practical suggestions that will give your Instagram account a boost and increase its popularity. Let me give you some tips that will "expose" your account.

- **Use your blog/website:** As an online entrepreneur, it is never out of line to believe that you either have a blog or a website used for promoting your business. You can expand the functionality of the website by using it to promote your Instagram account. If your website boasts a good volume of traffic, incorporate your Instagram account at strategic places in the website.

As more people come to read your posts, they will gradually become aware of your Instagram. If your account has some attractive and informative photos, you can rest assured knowing that some of your readers will take an interest in your Instagram account, thereby directly contributing to the growth of your Instagram account.

- **Promote with your complimentary card:** Your business card has an objective: get your business into the hands of as many people as possible. Over the years, it has been an effective promotional tool as well. You can extend its functions by using it to promote your Instagram account too. In addition to your phone number and email address, it is advisable that you include your Instagram account details on the card. As more people get the card, the better the chances of creating an even larger followership for your Instagram account.

- **Promote it with other tools:** Do you have office paraphernalia, or perhaps some giveaways? Promoting these items on Instagram is another avenue you can use to drive your followership through the roof. For instance, when you give your customers some giveaways, it promotes your brand to others who have not heard about your brand for one reason or another. It won't do you any harm if you decide to print your Instagram account details on these items. The more of these items that get into people's hands, the more awareness it will create for your brand. That may influence people and cause them to want to visit your page.

The combination of these tips will increase the visibility of your Instagram account drastically. Although the results may not be instant, the combination of other tips discussed in this book and your persistence will payout in dividends in the near future.

Have a complete bio

People won't take you seriously if your bio is incomplete. They will consider you as not serious enough to be followed. You can turn such a negative attitude around by filling in all the blanks in your profile. When filling out your bio, remember to use the most relevant hashtags and keywords to your brand, and make a link back to your brand website. While doing this, don't be tempted to be "spammy." If you are seen as a spammer, most Instagramers won't welcome your idea. That will mean a loss of potential followers. The rule is to be modest in your use of keywords and hashtags.

Remember that your bio will tell the viewers more information about your brand. This underlines the importance of making it as descriptive as possible. Let your bio contain relevant and useful information that other Instagram users can use to link with your business.

Updating your bio regularly in tune with any development in your brand, such as promoting any product or service, is a good way to ensure the completeness of your bio. If your bio is filled out but lacking in the most important areas, your audience won't find it useful. That is something that will ultimately defeat the objective of creating the account.

Add some emojis

Emojis quietly announced its arrival as the conventional means of expression on social media. The buzz surrounding it has not abated, and emojis have gained so much popularity over the years that they have become a powerful tool in the hands of expert social media users. A report by Instagram revealed that almost half of all the comments and captions on Instagram have emojis incorporated in them in order to have the right impact on other users. Here are some awesome facts about emojis that highlight their importance as a great tool for driving traffic to your account.

- The heart-shaped emoji (red) was announced in 2014. That year, it was used approximately 300 million times. That shows how popular it is. Due to the emotional feeling conveyed by this emoji, it is now widely used by Instagram users to attract people with similar emotions. You can use it for the same purpose on your Instagram photos as well.

- According to a study, there are some 800 emojis around the world. Over 90% of the online community is fond of using these emojis as a form of communicating with each other regularly. When a group of people was asked about their opinion on the use and accuracy of emojis as a means of expression, a whopping 84% of the women and an impressive 75% of the men answered in the affirmative.

The most widely used emojis are the happy faces. They are accountable for 45% of the total emojis used by Americans. What does this tell you?

The implication is that using emojis with your photo is one way to play on the emotional feelings of your users. Chances are that you will find a greater number of them respond to your photo according to the sentiment expressed by the emoji you used. Therefore, just as with the use of hashtags, find a convenient and effective ways to use emojis for a similar purpose to enlarge your Instagram's influence.

Emojis have gradually become a big deal. So, you shouldn't hesitate to use them to your advantage because with emojis, you can express your feelings better while you are still economical with words. While you are limited to a maximum of 160 characters on Instagram and always find it difficult to express your feelings or promote your brand within that limit, using emojis is a great way to express yourself without breaking the rules.

For instance, while the words "heartbreak" will take 10 characters, a single emoji will express the same feeling and save you those extra characters that you can then put to good use. That is the secret behind the popularity of emojis over the years.

Let your caption be catchy

After you have created a marvelous image or took a good photo, it is now time to showcase your images to the ever-increasing Instagram community. That can be challenging if you are a novice to the game. You may wonder how best to draw the attention of your potential follower and retain it. Although it requires some level of expertise to get it right, one of the most important and effective tips is to write a catchy caption for any of your photos. A catchy caption can make the difference between the success of your photo or its failure. Why?

This is due to the irrefutable fact that a catchy caption will prove irresistible for a user, drawing him or her to the picture. This will improve the engagement rate of the photo as people will be drawn to the picture, liking it, or commenting on it, depending on the level of its attractiveness and how catchy the caption is. Scores of studies have shown that catchy captions to have a powerful influence on consumers and users across different social media platforms. Some online business ideas, such as blogging, thrive on attractive captions for increased followership. The rules are the same for Instagram too.

Even if your photo has no caption or has a not-too-appealing caption, it will still be viewed by users, and giving it an attractive caption will make the difference. The number of visitors who will be attracted by the caption will be more than what you will get without an appealing caption.

Writing a catchy caption is the most challenging problem for some Instagram users. Many people cringe at the thought of having to do this. The good news is that writing a catchy caption for each of your photos does not require unique skills. You only need to know the rules and apply them. Some of the rules when writing a catchy caption include making your caption light and related to your photo. Then, don't forget the importance of using the right hashtag for each of your photos. Review the rules guiding the use of hashtags in Chapter 1 of this book to get it done right.

It can't be overemphasize enough, the importance of using the right caption for your pictures. It affords you the opportunity to draw attention to your post in the short-term. The long term impact includes more engagement that may eventually translate to increased conversion and the growth of your account. That will have a positive effect on your business or brand in the long run.

Remember that people are bound to engage in your photo if the caption is catchy. Some may be inclined to like the picture, tag a friend who may like it, or write meaningful comments about the photo. Others may decide to share the image too. All these can bring more viewers who may want to participate in commenting on your post. In the long run, it will get to more people than you could have convinced to join your campaign without such appealing captions.

Now think about this: How do photos go viral? Whenever a picture or a post goes viral, it is through the engagement of individuals to whom the picture speaks to. When your caption is catchy, there may be others who will feel so moved to share it. With each share, your chances of getting more value to your account increase each time a user clicks the share button. The more shares your photo can get the better result it will offer. And if you are fortunate to have a viral post, you will record unprecedented growth in your Instagram account. Your growth may hit the roof earlier than you expect.

Organize contests

Organizing contests is a brilliant way to increase your followership. When you organize a contest, you are creating awareness for your brand as more people get to know your page through the contest. That awareness will lead to increased popularity, more traffic, and a boost for your page ranking. The combination of these benefits will drive your page off the charts.

Organizing a good contest on Instagram is not challenging as some people will have you believe. You only need a good contest idea and the willingness to see it become a reality to reap the rich reward that comes with organizing one.

Since the platform has different contest options to choose from, choose the best option that will add value to your page and increase the popularity of your brand. Don't forget that the objective is to create a huge followership that will have a direct impact on your brand and sales.

Host a like-to-win contest

The role of likes in the growth of your page cannot be overemphasized. The more likes you get during this contest, the higher your reputation will soar. There is no better way to guarantee for yourself a floodgate of likes than by hosting a like-to-win contest. The technique is very simple and highly rewarding.

You simply need to upload an image about the contest on your page and ask people to like the image to win a prize. Then pick a winner at random when the contest ends.

Some practical tips that can help you achieve success with a contest include adding related industry tags to the image to capture the attention of your audience and the Instagram community at large. In addition to the hashtags that are related to your niche, two other important tags you shouldn't forget to include are #giveaway and #contest. These are valuable tags that will attract the community quickly. As a rule, your prize should be compelling. The result of this contest on your Instagram popularity will be awesome.

Now, let's get this straight. A one-off contest will have little impact on your page. However, a series of such contests will build impressive momentum for you. When you organize one contest after another, you will create buzz in the Instagram community, leading to repeated visits from Instagram users. As people have multiple chances to participate and win a contest, they will stop at nothing to win. That will lead to more likes, and when people have the opportunity to make repeated visits to your page to win a contest, your traffic will soar.

As a matter of fact, people will invite their friends, family members, or associates to participate in the contest as well, due to the prize they stand to gain if they win the contest. That will draw the attention of other users who are not already following you to get wind of it and participate. The more people that can participate in the contest, the better traffic you will get. It is in your interest to make the sharing and liking of the post a prerequisite for qualification for the contest. Imagine the powerful effect that 100 shares and 100 likes would have on your account.

It is never a bad idea to show the image of your company, business, or brand in the contest as a beginner. With time, you will learn about more effective ways to leverage the contest to increase your popularity without having the image of your brand splattered throughout the contest page.

Organizing a series of contests will give you more popularity and an increased follower base. All that at a ridiculously cheap cost!

To ensure that the contest delivers, live up to your promise and give winners what you promised. That will earn you the trust and respect of the participants and others who may be interested in future campaigns. With each contest, you will see the number of entrants increasing daily. Over time, your popularity will increase astronomically while your fan base will enjoy a similar increase in size.

Another useful tip is to make the contest user-generated. The contests, where users have the freedom to generate their ideas, are usually more popular and give room for more participants. Since everybody has equal chances of creating amazing user content, it is an effective way to draw in participants from the four walls of the Instagram community.

Make your first contest a memorable one. Let it serve as the promotional campaign for your subsequent ones. If your first contest lives up to its hype, getting sufficient participants in the next one will be easy. The participants in the first contest will be in high expectation of another contest while others, who were unaware of the first contest, may be impressed and willing to participate in subsequent ones. That will help you to slowly but gradually build up your fan base. Therefore, don't spare any effort to leave your participants with something to think of by the end of your first contest.

Launch a selfie contest

This contest is simply one of the best contests you could ever consider whenever you contemplate organizing a contest on Instagram. The reason is simple: people are passionate about taking selfies. Take advantage of that knowledge and organize a selfie contest to see people's response.

Since you want to use the contest to drive more traffic to your page and increase your fan base, use this simple rule: Let the contestants post selfie images of themselves with your product.

With a selfie contest, you have a great shot at making good use out of social media to promote your brand beyond imagination. It will increase your engagement with other users in the community, in addition to boosting your popularity.

Even if you are not promoting a physical product, you can still make the best use of selfie contests as others selling physical products can. Trust the participants to have their selfies posted on your page in addition to some other social media platforms. Expect them to have their selfies plastered on their other social media pages. You will have a tremendous turnout from the contestants.

The beauty of this contest is that users personally generate the content themselves. You can count on the creativity of the users to come up with different and attractive pictures that will win the hearts of other followers and the community at large. The selfie contest promises to be rewarding. When announcing the winner of a contest, you can create awareness for the next contest as a way of building anticipation for it.

Organize a hashtag contest

Hashtags have become one of the most powerful communication mediums on social media. Since people are adept at using them, create a contest around them.

A hashtag contest should require the contestants to post some photos and use the right hashtags in the images. Sometimes, you need to give them the hashtag you want to use. Then go through the hashtags to choose a winner.

This contest is an excellent one for branding purposes. It can help you to get your brand out there to the Internet community. As more and more contestants participate in the contest, you will easily build a good audience.

As is the common practice, you can set the rules for participating in the contest by asking users to share the post, like your page, and tag a friend. When these are effectively combined, more people will become aware of your post and that will mean more participation and engagement. That will assure you of a good outreach for your brand.

A voting contest is good

This contest saves you time and energy. You are not the judge but the Instagram community. When you organize this contest, you can ask your followers and others to submit their best photos to a specific hashtag you create for that specific purpose.

To increase the engagement, ask other people to be the judge by voting for the best picture through comments and likes. To narrow down the effect of the contest, you can make the participants post the photo of anything related to your business.

Since the Internet community will play all the roles - participating in the contest and judging - it offers the community an excellent way to contribute to your growth. That in essence, means that more people will get involved in the contest from the beginning to the end. The likes, comments, contests, and shares will give you the best results. More people will get to know about your page, especially when contestants are required to tag their friends or share the post to qualify for the contest.

Follow other people

You are not the only one in the social community. The community survives when people "follow" one another. That keeps the cycle going. While you expect others to follow you while building your portfolio, some people have the same goal too; they want to build their accounts and have the same passion as you. Since respect is reciprocal, the unwritten rule in social media is that you follow someone who follows you. Although this is an unwritten rule, many people in the social media community have learned to respect and obey this rule. Don't dare to be the exception.

However, the rule doesn't stipulate that you must follow every person in the social media community. That would be excessive and contrary to your goals, but is important that you find related and appealing pages to follow.

When you follow others, like their pages and comment on them. Engage meaningfully in their posts and see the results come back on your page. It is natural for them to appreciate and return the favor. If you follow about 500 people, some hundreds of these people may decide to follow you as well. That will give them unhindered access to your new posts and thus contribute their own little quota to the growth of your page through personal engagements and contributions. You can't underestimate the potential for growth that is hidden in your new followers.

You can get them more involved in your campaign by doing

these things. Visit their pages, likes the posts that you find appealing, and leave meaningful comments whenever that is necessary. That will go a long way to establishing a good relationship between you and your followers. That's the best way to get them involved with your brand.

Update your account regularly

Cultivating the habit of updating your account regularly is one of the most effective ways to drive your traffic up. A series of studies have shown a correlation exists between updating your posts and getting more conversion on social media sites. From LinkedIn to Twitter, Facebook and Instagram, the story remains the same.

The principle behind this is not that far-fetched. People will be attracted by relevant and up-to-date information rather than waste their time reading stale news. How would you feel if you visited someone's page daily for about a week or two but you still found the same information throughout that time? That may kill any interest you have in the person or the brand, if it is a brand. That's the feeling of most people.

On Instagram and elsewhere, people are captivated by fresh information everyday while they are appalled by stale information. They will always be looking forward to seeing more of your posts if you have a reputation for updating your account regularly.

Some research stipulated that the best practice is to update your page about 2 to 3 times a day. If you can do that regularly, you will gradually but consistently, build your fan base. A study conducted by Quilty supported this assertion.

This analytics tool that is designed for analyzing social media analyzed the profiles of over 5,000 users in 2015 to determine the impact of growth in regards to the number of posts on a page. The result of the analysis shows that these Instagram accounts with impressive fan bases have a reputation for posting a minimum of two posts daily.

So, it can be concluded that the more you are committed to feeding your readers with valuable information via your photos daily, the stronger their determination will be to always check your posts for updated information about your business. Note however, that the emphasis is not on the quantity of your post but the quality. Give them a good dose of quality posts a couple of times a day and you will benefit immensely.

Rather than feed people with posts that add no value to them, and if it doesn't add any promotional value to your business, have the mind of posting pictures that will promote your brand and will equally be attractive enough for your audience. So, you must combine quality posting with regular posting for the best results. Brands that have created the culture out of updating their accounts regularly can boast of the better results than brands that do their updating sporadically.

In imitation of Facebook, Instagram is ready to roll out another feature that will reward the regular updating of one's account. The feature focuses on rewarding individuals that update their accounts regularly with more visibility, just as Facebook does.

If you update regularly and your posts are shared by your fans, Instagram will use the information to rank you high and on the top of your fans' feeds. That will automatically have a tremendous effect on your user engagement and popularity.

Invite your users to tag a friend

This is another trick that can perform wonders. Have you ever thought of asking your followers to tag a friend to a particular post? Let me narrate an experience by a company that used the method effectively to drive its fan base. According to the company, "I recently got a great Instagram tip from some new local friends who helped me out with marketing a non-profit food tasting event. They shared a food photo from a past event and asked their 11,000 followers to comment and **tag a friend they wanted to attend with**. The response was awesome, and exposed our event to a lot of people who wouldn't have heard about it otherwise."

You can do the same. Now, you can get the best opportunity to promote your brand with this simple but highly effective tip. How does it work?

Let's assume you have just 100 followers. Asking each of them to tag a friend will give you some results, perhaps 70 or 80%. If 80 people decide to tag a friend each, that will be another 80 viewers. What happens if those tagged decide to extend the game by tagging others who they feel your post will be useful for? Over time, many people will become aware of your account. Depending on how frequently you update your account and the quality of your post, you will gain a lot popularity in a short time.

Using this method effectively is very easy. The success lies in your personal commitment to the cause. It is important to constantly share captivating and beautiful photos that will be easily noticed and that can compel them to act. That will assure you the constant visiting of your followers.

Cross-promote your page

The Internet has an abundance of social media platforms. We have Facebook, Twitter, Instagram, and Snapchat, not to mention several others. Although this book is directed towards Instagram, it can also be used in conjunction with other platforms to promote your brand and increase your business awareness.

You can leverage the billions of users on these platforms to create awareness for your brand by promoting your Instagram photos on other platforms. By sharing your photos on the other platforms, you expand your horizon and give better room for your brand to be more visible to others outside of Instagram. For instance, if you have a highly engaging post on your Instagram account, it is beneficial to share such photos on Foursquare, Flickr, Tumblr, Facebook, and Twitter.

While Instagram alone can boast of giving you some millions of users, the combination of these platforms will give you exposure to billions of users from all walks of life. There is the tendency that the more your photos are shared across these platforms, the more people that will get to know about you. What's more? People who find your photos valuable to them may also assist you by sharing your photos. That will contribute to the growth of your Instagram followership in a big way. This offers you the needed exposure at no cost.

The free exposure offered by these people and platforms will boost your chances of getting the desired popularity, especially if your photos meet the basic requirements: good quality and attractive.

In addition to sharing your Instagram posts on these platforms, you can take advantage of another feature

Facebook has. The social media giant creates room for Instagram users to embed some of their Instagram posts on their Facebook pages. What does that mean for you? Depending on your activity on the platform, you can enjoy unprecedented popularity due to the larger number of users on Facebook, compared to other platforms.

You can also take your cross-promoting to your blog too. If you have a blog, that is another platform that can increase your popularity faster than you can ever imagine. You can devote a section of your blog to your Instagram activities or embed a couple of your Instagram posts into some relevant posts to further your cause.

It is crucial to your success that you understand the importance of having good traffic on your blog before you can derive the rewards. That will facilitate your Instagram growth rate.

Don't forget to create awareness about the existence of your Instagram page on other social media platforms where you have a valid account. Post a link to your account on all of these platforms and see the positive results that it will generate.

A couple of years ago, Buzzsumo conducted a study to determine the effectiveness of promoting an Instagram account on different platforms on the growth rate of the account. What was the result?

After studying more than 1 billion Facebook posts belonging to over 3 million Facebook users, the company came to the conclusion that the engagement rate of an image increased if it was posted to Facebook via Instagram than if it is posted directly onto Facebook. The implication is that you can are guaranteed more success with the Instagram account if you promote your photos across multiple platforms. This is good news if you are contemplating widening out with Facebook and other platforms.

Don't forget however, that people won't be interested in following you if your account is inactive or has little content to offer. You will defeat your cross-promotion goal if you don't meet these basic requirements.

Made in the USA
Middletown, DE
27 March 2018